WINTER SOLDIER
IRAQ AND AFGHANISTAN

WINTER SOLDIER
IRAQ AND AFGHANISTAN
EYEWITNESS ACCOUNTS
OF THE OCCUPATIONS

Iraq Veterans Against the War
and
Aaron Glantz

Photographs by Jared Rodriguez and Mike Hastie

Haymarket Books
Chicago, Illinois

Published in 2008 by Haymarket Books
P.O. Box 180165
Chicago, IL 60618
773-583-7884
info@haymarketbooks.org
www.haymarketbooks.org

Cover and interior testifier portraits by Jared Rodriguez
Additional photographs by Mike Hastie, including testifier portraits on pages 38, 74, 89, 124, 138,
    140, 167, 169, 182, 209
Cover design by Eric Ruder
Book design by David Whitehouse

Published with the generous support of the Wallace Global Fund.

Trade distribution:
In the U.S. through Consortium Book Sales and Distribution, www.cbsd.com
In the UK, Turnaround Publisher Services, www.turnaround-psl.com
In Australia, Palgrave MacMillan, www.palgravemacmillan.com.au
All other countries, Publishers Group Worldwide, www.pgw.com/home/worldwide.aspx

Special discounts are available for bulk purchases by organizations and institutions. Please contact
Haymarket Books for more information at 773-583-7884 or info@haymarketbooks.org.

Printed in Canada by union labor on recycled paper containing 100 percent post-consumer waste
in accordance with the guidelines of the Green Press Initiative, www.greenpressinitiative.org

LIBRARY OF CONGRESS CATALOGING-IN-PUBLICATION DATA
Iraq Veterans Against the War.
  Winter soldier, Iraq and Afghanistan : eyewitness accounts of the occupations / Iraq Veterans
Against the War and Aaron Glantz.
    p. cm.
  ISBN 978-1-931859-65-3 (pbk.)
  1. Iraq War, 2003---Personal narratives, American. 2. Afghan War, 2001---Personal narratives,
American. I. Glantz, Aaron. II. Title.
  DS79.76.I7272 2008
  956.7044'3092273--dc22
                            2008036840

10 9 8 7 6 5 4 3 2 1

CONTENTS

We dedicate this book to good people of Iraq and Afghanistan who know the veracity of these stories.

And to all the servicemembers and veterans who never had a chance to tell their stories.

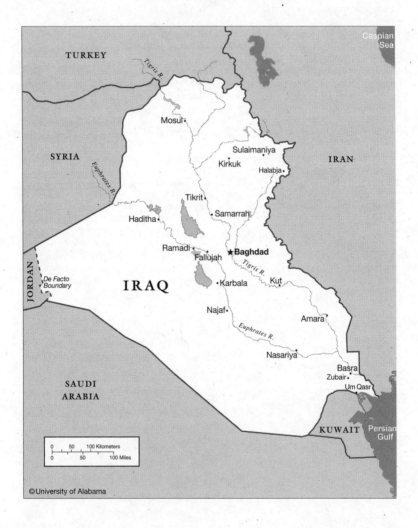

FOREWORD

Anthony Swofford

Early in June of 2008 President Bush awarded the Bronze Star posthumously to Specialist Ross A. McGinnis of the United States Army. McGinnis had done what most civilians would find unthinkable: he'd jumped on an enemy hand grenade that had been thrown into his vehicle. His body took the force of the entire blast and he died instantly, saving four fellow soldiers from certain heinous injury and probable death. His was the selfless act popularized in the culture by Hollywood lore and the macho love talk of tough men: I'd take a bullet for you; I'd jump on a grenade to save so-and-so's life. No one ever means it. But men and women in battle do. It's not in any manual. It's written in the code of the combatant's heart. It's the kind of impulse that is part of the reason most people join the United States military in the first place: to serve, to honor, to protect.

The men and women who testified at Winter Soldier Iraq and Afghanistan in March of 2008 displayed the same kind of courage that Specialist McGinnis did: they took individual action and great risk to honor the men and women, American troops and Iraqi civilians, who have died in this misbegotten and often criminally executed war. They didn't use their bodies; they used their narratives, the bare-knuckle stories that tell us the truth about what happens at the other end of the rifle, the missile, the bomb.

I listened to most of the testimony live that weekend. Despite my service in the Marine Corps during the 1990–1991 Gulf War and my intimate knowledge of the brutality of combat and the systems that prepare one for combat, there were times during the testimony when I found myself in utter disbelief. I call combat a psychosis-inducing situation. But still, the events being narrated by the testifying troops shocked me. You too will be shocked. Your natural tendency will be not to believe.

It will be hard to imagine the same kind of sweet young kid you went to high school with or that your sons or daughters went to high school with telling about warships firing on civilian-inhabited apartment buildings while troops cheer the destruction; it will be difficult to believe the blind blood-thirst a unit lives and kills on after suffering casualties; you do not want to know about the constantly loosening Rules of Engagement that eventually debilitate to the point of allowing troops to shoot anyone who makes them feel unsafe. You won't want to believe the "incentivizing" one marine captain does: be the first to kill with a knife and you'll get some extra days off when the unit rotates home.

Tim O'Brien has written that in a war story, the craziest stuff in there—the events a civilian would never believe because they are filled with such violence and depravity—those are the true parts of the story. These are what I call the seared elements: the images and associated narratives of a combatant's history he or she most wants to forget but never will. In this testimony there are countless seared elements that you the reader will want to forget.

But honor the casualties of this war—the dead, injured, psychologically altered, those who have already managed to heal—by refusing to forget the elements and consequences of combat that our leaders would rather us not know in the first place. Do not turn away from these stories. They are yours, too.

June 2008

MESSAGE FROM KELLY DOUGHERTY

Executive Director of Iraq Veterans Against the War

Kelly Dougherty served in Iraq from March 2003 until February 2004 as a medic in a military police unit of the Colorado National Guard. She is one of the original founders of IVAW and currently serves as its executive director.

In the winter of 2002 I was working in a café and preparing to finish my bachelor's degree at the University of Colorado. The U.S. government's threats toward Iraq were growing and there was more and more anticipation of a war being an inevitable, foregone conclusion. While I was working, I wore a pin on my apron that said, "Attack Iraq?! NO!" One day a customer looked at my pin, scoffed, and said, "It's more like, Iraq, don't attack us!" While being opposed to a war against Iraq from the beginning, and highly skeptical of the information flowing out of the White House and major news outlets, I still felt detached and not overly concerned about the prospect of war. Yes, I was a sergeant in the Colorado Army National Guard, but I was in a headquarters unit, we didn't get deployed.

Looking back, this attitude was not only naive, but also selfish. Today the pervasiveness of just such an ambivalent, flippant attitude maddens me. I would soon experience in a very real way just how political decisions have a personal impact on people's lives. In January 2003 I received a call from the National Guard informing me that I had been transferred from my "safe" unit into a military police unit that was getting mobilized to active duty status the next day and would be deploying to Kuwait in preparation for the war. What's more, my military job had been changed from medic to military police.

I deployed with my unit in February of 2003, was in Kuwait for the initial invasion, and then moved north into Iraq. I spent nearly a year patrolling Southern Iraq, escorting U.S. corporate convoys, and anticipating the day I would return home. While my experience in Iraq was difficult, stressful, and confusing, my unit brought everyone home alive and I consider myself extremely fortunate to be intact. The experience of being an armed occupier in an unknown, foreign country, and the impact that the war and occupation of Iraq had and will continue to have for generations, led me to make a decision to try to become a proactive force in effecting positive change.

●   ●   ●

My father is a navy Vietnam-era veteran who joined Veterans for Peace (VFP) in 2003. He hated seeing me deploy to Iraq and even visited the country himself as part of a delegation during the first year of the occupation. Soon after my return home from Iraq, my father invited me to attend the VFP convention that July in Boston. I was excited at the opportunity but had no idea what to expect. To my surprise, I arrived to find out that I'd been scheduled to speak on a panel with several other veterans who'd served in Iraq and the Middle East. I was nervous and had no idea what to say. One of the other vets told me to "speak from the heart." While I found this advice corny, I think what he was really saying was, "speak from your experience." As I've come to learn, there is nothing more powerful or engaging than one's own personal story.

Several of the Iraq veterans at the convention had been discussing with VFP their desire to form an organization made up of post–9/11 vets that opposed the Iraq war. They wanted to give a voice to the opposition within the ranks of those serving in the "Global War on Terror." Our mentors in Veterans for Peace were very supportive and on July 24, 2004, Michael Hoffman, Alex Ryabov, Tim Goodrich, Jimmy Massey, Diana Morrison, and I stood on stage at historic Faneuil Hall alongside military family members, and announced the formation of Iraq Veterans Against the War (IVAW).

Those of us in Boston, as well as other early members of IVAW, were all on our own paths toward understanding and finding meaning in our military and wartime experiences. We implicitly understood the value of veterans' and servicemembers' voices in the discussion about Iraq and foreign policy, and knew that we had a very important role to play. From the beginning, the goals of Iraq Veterans Against the War were clear:

An immediate, unconditional withdrawal of all occupying forces from Iraq;

Health care and other benefits for all veterans and servicemembers;

Reparations to the Iraqi people.

Our members consist of women and men who've served in the U.S. military since September 11, 2001, and are united by our goals or three points of unity. We are strategically organizing within the military and veteran communities to build and support opposition to the ongoing occupation, as well as educate the public about the true human costs of war. We believe that those who have taken part in death, destruction, and trauma can transform their experiences to build a more just, peaceful world.

• • •

As our membership began to grow, and chapters began to form, IVAW entered a new level of organizing and strategizing on how to be an effective force to be reckoned with. We organized Winter Soldier Iraq and Afghanistan in part because our members see the history and day-to-day narration of the Iraq occupation being told and remembered by politicians, generals, pundits, and corporate media. The voices, experiences, and opinions of those most affected, the Iraqis, the servicemembers, and military families, are often marginalized or ignored. IVAW members seek to challenge the assumption that only those with wealth or power can write history or lend crucial insight to the life-and-death issues that affect us all. The members of IVAW show courage, conviction, and integrity as they continue to raise their voices in support of human dignity and freedom, and in opposition to the degrading forces of war and occupation that dehumanize and destroy their fellow human beings.

The current volume, *Winter Soldier Iraq and Afghanistan: Eyewitness Accounts of the Occupations*, is based on the biggest event that IVAW has organized to date. The hearings, held at the National Labor College, in Silver

Spring, Maryland between March 13 and 16, 2008, gathered more than two hundred veterans of the two conflicts and featured testimony from veterans, Iraqi civilians, military families, and others. The event helped to build the leadership of our members, strengthening the relationships among them across the country, while providing a painful glimpse into the brutality of the occupation. One of the most poignant findings of the hearings is that the abuses committed in the occupations, far from being the result of a "few bad apples" misbehaving, are the result of our government's Middle East policy, which is crafted in the highest spheres of U.S. power. The behavior of the troops on the ground is an inseparable part of our military occupation, and the toll that is taken on the civilians and soldiers who suffer through this sort of institutionalized mass violence is nearly impossible to comprehend.

Our members' testimony helped set the record straight and created an important tool for the American people to challenge the official government line. While at Winter Soldier, I had members tell me that they finally felt part of a national movement. One member told me that he felt more proud of his work with IVAW than of his entire service in the Marine Corps. IVAW means more to its members than making a political statement. Our organization represents healing, reclaiming pieces of ourselves that we thought were lost, atoning for our role in the suffering of others, and continuing to help each other and stand up for our country. Once we began the collection of testimony for Winter Soldier, more and more members wanted to submit their first-hand accounts. We plan to make the collection of Winter Soldier testimony an ongoing part of IVAW's work in order to document our own history as an organization and as a group of people who are intimately aware of the impacts of war.

• • •

When I was in Iraq, I often thought of the saying, "What doesn't kill you makes you stronger." Although it is a cliché, it helped me and I think there is truth in it. We've survived bullets, IEDs, scorching heat, bitter cold, intimidation, harassment, and attacks, and yet we continue with renewed determination and focus. We know the value and impact that our personal stories carry and that is what Winter Soldier Iraq and Afghanistan is all about: opening up a space for veterans and servicemembers to share their stories firsthand.

Speaking openly and candidly about our experiences at war, in the military, and as returning vets, however, is not a simple task. When we relive traumatic moments we open ourselves up for criticism, we remember things we'd rather forget, we take a risk. But when we speak up, when we share our stories, we also open up the possibility of healing, bit by bit, from our trauma. When we find and exercise our voices, we start to realize the power that we have inside us, the power that, when organized and solidified, can do amazing things, like end occupations. We never fully know the impact that we have when we find the strength to speak out. Our voices resonate to unexpected places and give hope, solace, inspiration, and motivation to people we will never meet.

When we return home from combat, many people would rather not hear our stories, would rather not be made to feel uncomfortable by being confronted with the grim reality of warfare and occupation, where morality becomes obscured and the lines between good and bad are fluid and hazy. By acknowledging our experiences, it pressures people to recognize their own responsibility for the actions being taken by a military that is ultimately meant to defend them. It is often much easier for people to call us heroes and forget about us, forget about the sacrifices we've made and horrors we've endured. We must remind people that the occupations in Iraq and Afghanistan are being waged by the United States as a country, not simply by our military or our political administration. By speaking out, we pressure our fellow Americans to acknowledge their own responsibility for these occupations, which is a necessary part in bringing them to an end.

IVAW continues to move forward, carrying the message of Winter Soldier, more powerful and united than ever before. We've asserted IVAW as an effective, focused group that has a strategy to end the occupation of Iraq. We are leading the GI and veteran movement to bring our brothers and sisters home now, and we're to be taken seriously and treated with respect. We are writing history from the point of view of those who've lived through these occupations and experienced the on-the-ground reality. We are proud, we are committed, we are 1,300 strong and growing, and we will keep fighting for each other.

INTRODUCTION

I n 1777 the United States was on the verge of losing the War of Independence. George Washington's troops had suffered a string of defeats and had to retreat to Valley Forge, Pennsylvania, where they suffered through a brutally cold winter. Undernourished and poorly clothed, two thousand soldiers died of typhus, typhoid, dysentery, and pneumonia. Others began to desert.

Even Washington worried that he might have to give up. "Unless some great and capital change suddenly takes place," he wrote, "...This Army must inevitably...starve, dissolve, or disperse, in order to obtain subsistence in the best manner they can."[1]

But the words of the great revolutionary Thomas Paine rallied the troops. "These are the times that try men's souls," Paine wrote. "The summer soldier and the sunshine patriot will, in this crisis, shrink from the service of their country; but he that stands by it now, deserves the love and thanks of man and woman. Tyranny, like hell, is not easily conquered; yet we have this consolation with us, that the harder the conflict, the more glorious the triumph."

Members of Iraq Veterans Against the War said they were showing that kind of courage when they gathered in March 2008 at the National Labor College in Silver Spring, Maryland to talk about what they saw and did while deployed overseas. They called the event Winter Soldier Iraq and Afghanistan: Eyewitness Accounts of the Occupations.

Over four days of gripping testimony, dozens of veterans spoke about

6

killing innocent civilians, randomly seizing and torturing prisoners, refusing to treat injured Afghans and Iraqis, looting, taking "trophy" photos of the dead, and falsifying reports to make it look as though civilians they killed were actually "insurgents." Their goal: to show that high-profile atrocities like the torture of prisoners inside Abu Ghraib and the massacre of twenty-four innocent civilians at Haditha were not isolated incidents perpetrated by a "few bad apples," but part of a pattern of increasingly bloody occupations.

They also demonstrated, by relating their firsthand experiences, how the military occupation of a foreign country inevitably leads to an increase in racism, dehumanization, and sexism directed both outward at the enemy and inward into the soul of the servicemember. Many of the veterans who testified apologized to their peers and to the American and Iraqi people. Others (and sometimes these were the same veterans) used their testimony to try to break their fellow citizens out of a collective apathy that allows the war and occupation to continue.

"These are the consequences for sending young men and women to battle," former Marine Corps Rifleman Vincent Emanuele said in one of Winter Soldier's opening panels. "What I'd like to ask anyone who's witnessing this, or anyone who's viewing this testimony, is to imagine your loved ones put in such positions. Your brothers, your sisters, your nieces, your nephews, your aunts, and your uncles, and more importantly, and maybe most importantly, to be able to put ourselves in the Iraqis' shoes who encountered these events every day and for the last five years."

In organizing Winter Soldier, IVAW took its inspiration from Vietnam Veterans Against the War (VVAW), which organized a precedent-setting gathering in 1971 in Detroit. At that time, the United States had reached a point in the Vietnam War very similar to the Iraq War in 2007. Public opinion had moved decidedly against the war, coalition partners like Australia and New Zealand were withdrawing their troops, and the *Pentagon Papers*, which had just been released, documented a long history of official lies. And yet the war continued, as President Richard Nixon pushed ahead with an expansion of U.S. intervention in Southeast Asia, which included the invasion of Cambodia.

Vietnam Veterans Against the War were determined to play a role in changing the course of the war. They gathered in Detroit to explain what they had really done while deployed overseas in service of their country.

They showed, through first-person testimony, that atrocities like the My Lai massacre were not isolated exceptions.

"[The 1971] Winter Soldier heralded a significant change of opinion in the American public toward Vietnam veterans," wrote historian Gerald Niccosia in *Home to War: A History of the Vietnam Veterans Movement*, "not only in terms of a new willingness to hear their side of things, but also in the amount of respect and credibility they were accorded."[2]

Over a dozen members of Congress endorsed the gathering. Senator George McGovern of South Dakota and Congressman John Conyers of Michigan called for full congressional investigations into charges leveled by the veterans at the Winter Soldier hearings. Three months later, twenty-seven-year-old Navy Lieutenant John Kerry, who had served on a Swift boat in Vietnam, took VVAW's case to Congress and spoke before a jammed Senate Foreign Relations Committee hearing. Television cameras lined the walls and veterans packed the seats.

"Many very highly decorated veterans testified to war crimes committed in Southeast Asia," Kerry told the committee, describing the events of the Winter Soldier gathering. "It is impossible to describe to you exactly what did happen in Detroit—the emotions in the room, and the feelings of the men who were reliving their experiences in Vietnam. They relived the absolute horror of what this country, in a sense, made them do."

In one of the most famous antiwar speeches of the era, Kerry concluded, "Someone has to die so that President Nixon won't be—and these are his words—'the first president to lose a war.' We are asking Americans to think about that, because how do you ask a man to be the last man to die in Vietnam? How do you ask a man to be the last man to die for a mistake?"[3]

Members of Iraq Veterans Against the War hoped that Winter Soldier Iraq and Afghanistan would play a similarly historic role. So far, however, they've run up against indifference at high levels of Congress and the corporate media. Though the March 2008 gathering was timed to coincide with the fifth anniversary of the invasion of Iraq and was held in Silver Spring, Maryland, less than ten miles from the White House, the personal testimony of hundreds of Iraq and Afghanistan war veterans garnered scant coverage. The *Washington Post* buried an article on Winter Soldier Iraq and Afghanistan in the Metro section. The *New York Times*, CNN, ABC, NBC, and CBS ignored it completely.

Winter Soldier Iraq and Afghanistan did garner interest from the foreign press and military publications including *Stars and Stripes* and *Army Times*. Winter Soldier also caught the eyes of members of the Congressional Progressive Caucus, and on May 15, 2008, the caucus invited nine veterans to speak on Capitol Hill. "We now have an opportunity to hear not from the military's top brass but directly from you," Caucus Co-chair Congresswoman Lynn Woolsey of California said, "the very soldiers who put your lives on the line to carry out this president's failed policies."

Again, the vast majority of mainstream media outlets passed on covering the Progressive Caucus forum on Winter Soldier, and, as of this writing, no standing committee of the House or Senate has extended an invitation to IVAW like the one extended to John Kerry in 1971 by the Senate Foreign Relations Committee and its prestigious chair, William Fulbright.

Members of IVAW find these developments upsetting but not discouraging. Many say it's more important to organize within the ranks of the military than inside the halls of Congress. Many observers believe the army is already close to its breaking point. In February 2008, General George Casey, the Army chief of staff, said, "The cumulative effects of the last six-plus years at war have left our Army out of balance."[4]

Casey told the Senate Armed Services Committee that cutting the time soldiers spend in combat is an integral part of reducing the stress on the force. In 2007, Senate Republicans and President George W. Bush sabotaged Democratic attempts to ensure troops as much rest time at home as they'd spent on their most recent tour overseas. Cycling troops through three or four tours in Iraq and Afghanistan has been the only way Bush has been able to maintain a force of more than 140,000 U.S. soldiers in Iraq. Many of IVAW's most active members are veterans who served one tour in Iraq and then filed for conscientious-objector status or went AWOL to avoid a second deployment.

"We don't need to rely on the mainstream media," said Aaron Hughes, a former Illinois National Guardsman who drove convoys in Iraq. "We're building up this community that's saying: 'I don't have to follow these illegal orders. I do have a voice. And you know what, I'm not going to let a politician or a general or the media speak for me anymore. Let me tell you what's really going on.'" Hughes added, "Let's have those conversations in public, and together as a community we can end this war, because you know what—when the soldiers stop fighting this war, the war's over."

In the two months following Winter Soldier, IVAW increased its membership by 25 percent. Veterans around the country began holding smaller, mini-Winter Soldiers at which soldiers who had been unable to travel to Washington were able to tell their stories. Despite the media blackout, the grim reality of the occupations of Iraq and Afghanistan is leaching out into the broader populace. Increasingly, veterans and active-duty members of the Armed Forces get reinforcement that they are not alone.

Indeed, immediately following the Congressional Progressive Caucus hearing, U.S. Army Sergeant Matthis Chiroux announced he was refusing orders to deploy to Iraq in July. Chiroux said the idea of a deployment to Iraq initially made him suicidal. "I just went into my room and shut the door and barely emerged for close to a month. I just sat in my room reading news about Iraq and feeling completely hopeless, like I would be forced to go and no one would ever know how I felt. I was getting looped into participating in a crime against humanity and all with the realization that I never wanted to be there in the first place."

The turning point, Chiroux said, came when one of his professors at Brooklyn College in New York suggested he listen to a broadcast of March's Winter Soldier hearings.

"Here's an organization of soldiers and veterans who feel like me," he said. "All this alienation and depression that I feel started to ease. I found them, and I've been speaking out with them ever since."

A Note on the Testimony:

The text of *Winter Soldier Iraq and Afghanistan: Eyewitness Accounts of the Occupations* comes from testimony offered by veterans in Silver Spring, Maryland, from March 13 to 16, 2008, and in front of the Congressional Progressive Caucus on May 15, 2008. Due to space constraints, this book does not represent an exhaustive preparation of all the information presented at either gathering. Each testimony has been edited and a few of the testifiers could not be accommodated. Complete video archives of every veteran's testimony are available on Iraq Veterans Against the War's website, www.ivaw.org. Complete audio archives are available at www.warcomeshome.org.

Each veteran who testified at Winter Soldier went through an extensive verification before they were allowed to testify. A team of veterans and journalists collected documentation of every testifier's proof of service, including their military discharge papers (DD214s), ID cards, and corroborating evidence to support their stories. Photos, videos, military orders, Standard Operating Procedures, Rules of Engagement cards, and anything else the testifier could provide was collected in the testifier's file. Veterans and journalists also contacted testifiers' battle buddies (people they served with) and located media reports that corresponded with the dates, locations, and units the testifiers mentioned in their stories. We placed a stringent burden of proof on testifiers to demonstrate that they were deployed when and where they said they were.

IVAW and Aaron Glantz
August 2008

RULES OF ENGAGEMENT

Former marine Sergio Kochergin: "As the casualties grew in number, the rules became lenient. Because we saw our friends getting blown up and killed every day, we didn't really question them. We were angry. We just wanted to do our job and come back."

PHOTO: MIKE HASTIE

INTRODUCTION

War causes death. There's no way around that, but over hundreds of years, the Law of War has developed. These internationally agreed-upon standards set out what legally can and cannot be done by soldiers deployed into battle. These laws are designed to keep soldiers on both sides safe from torture and ill treatment and to ensure that innocent civilians are not killed unnecessarily.

These standards, which are set down in the Geneva Conventions, require warring parties to distinguish between lawful military targets and unlawful civilian ones. The Law of War specifically forbids attacks on hospitals, schools, places of worship, and other central parts of the civilian infrastructure. Direct, intentional attacks on noncombatants are also prohibited.

Servicemen and women learn these rules in training, and when they're deployed into battle they receive more specific Rules of Engagement that state what is and is not permitted given the mission at hand. In the Iraq War, the Rules of Engagement were initially quite restrictive.

"Do not target or strike any of the following except in self-defense: ... civilians, hospitals, mosques, national monuments, and any other historical and cultural sites," reads the Rules of Engagement card given to soldiers and marines in January 2003, before the invasion of Iraq.

Do not fire into civilian populated areas or buildings unless the enemy is using them for military purposes or if necessary for your self-defense. ...

13

Minimize collateral damage. Do not target enemy infrastructure (public works, commercial communication facilities, dams), Lines of Communication (roads, highways, tunnels, bridges, railways) and Economic Objects (commercial storage facilities, pipelines) unless necessary for self-defense or if ordered by your commander. If you must fire on these objects to engage a hostile force, disable and disrupt but avoid destruction of these objects, if possible.[1]

Those Rules of Engagement were not always followed, but initially they were widely respected and, as a result, civilian casualties were kept to a minimum. Once Saddam Hussein was overthrown, however, an armed resistance erupted against the U.S. occupation. With the Iraqi army defeated, many Iraqi civilians became involved as "insurgents"—Iraqis who dressed in regular civilian clothing and lived in civilian homes and apartment buildings with their families. They dropped their children off at school, went to work, and then after work spotted mortar rounds, buried roadside bombs, and fired rocket-propelled grenades at American soldiers.

Tailors, barbers, and car mechanics joined militias that attacked U.S. troops. Every Iraqi person was a potential insurgent. "Major combat operations" had been declared over, but by June 2003, American soldiers were being attacked over a thousand times a day. The military command structure responded to these developments by loosening the Rules of Engagement significantly. For most of the five-year-long occupation of Iraq, ROE has required American soldiers only to identify a "hostile act" or "hostile intent" before firing a weapon.[2]

As you'll see in the testimony that follows, commanders have interpreted these terms very loosely. Hospitals, mosques, schools, and historic sites have all been targeted. Shootings of innocents at checkpoints and during house raids and convoy operations are excused. From 2003 to 2006, the *Washington Post* reports, only thirty-nine service members were formally accused in connection with the deaths of Iraqis. Just twelve of the accused served prison time, none of them officers.[3]

Innocent Iraqi civilians are not killed in a vacuum. Their deaths are not limited to a few headline-grabbing events like the killing of twenty-four civilians in Haditha on November 19, 2005. Iraqi civilians are killed every day, their deaths an unavoidable part of guerilla war in general and this occupation in particular. An example of this is in the way the command structure responds to specific cases in which civilians are killed—not the big cases spotlighted in the media, but the everyday killings most Americans never hear about.

In September 2007 the American Civil Liberties Union obtained nearly ten thousand pages of previously classified U.S. Army documents, which show how the government responds to civilian casualties. The court-martial proceedings and military investigations reveal that the definitions of "hostile intent" and "hostile actions" are so broad that virtually any activity by an Iraqi can be used to justify the use of force.

One army document describes a November 12, 2005, incident in Abu Saida, northeast of Baghdad.[4] According to the document, an Iraqi driver was "killed (shot) by American soldiers at a checkpoint after being turned back.... While attempting to turn around, an American soldier shot him. The other three passengers took him to the hospital where he was later pronounced dead."

Six months later, on March 25, 2006, a judge advocate captain at Forward Operating Base Warhorse completed his investigation (the captain's name is redacted in the document). "There is insufficient evidence to prove US negligence or wrongful act," it reads. "Such fire engagement by any checkpoint guardsman was likely a result of the deceased's failure to follow written or verbal instruction at a checkpoint."

Another document describes an incident that took place on December 2, 2005. "Claimant stated her husband was shot and killed by CF (Coalition Forces) while driving produce from his farm to sell at the market. Claimant also stated that CF brought her husband's body to her house."

Six weeks later, on January 12, 2006, a judge advocate captain exonerated the soldiers. There was no "negligent or wrongful acts of military members or civilian employees of the Armed Forces," he wrote. "The shooting was lawful as it was initiated only after the victim demonstrated hostile intent by pulling into the middle of the convoy."

According to research published in the prestigious British medical journal *The Lancet*, approximately 186,000 Iraqis were killed by U.S. troops and their coalition allies between March 2003 and July 2006.[5] Researchers from Johns Hopkins University, MIT, and Mustansuriye University in Baghdad traveled to all eighteen provinces of Iraq, used a GPS system, and randomly visited nearly two thousand households. To date, their casualty count is the only systematic effort to survey the number of civilian dead since the war began. Some have criticized their methods and said the estimate is unreasonably high. As you read through the Winter Soldier testimony on the Rules of Engagement and experience the occupation as lived by these veterans, remember that the killing they describe is the result of official policy, a natural outgrowth of the U.S. occupation of Iraq.

JASON WAYNE LEMIEUX

Sergeant, United States Marine Corps, Infantry

Deployments:
January 2003–September 2003, Karbala
February 2004–September 2004, Husaybah
September 2005–March 2006, al-Ramadi

Hometown: Anaheim, California

Age at Winter Soldier: 25 years old

During the invasion of Iraq, during the push north to Baghdad, the Rules of Engagement given to me were gradually reduced to nonexistence. When we first crossed the Kuwait-Iraq border at Azubad in March 2003, we were operating under Geneva Convention guidelines and, with the exception of medical and religious personnel, we were authorized to shoot anyone wearing a military uniform unless they had surrendered.

By the time we got to Baghdad, however, I was explicitly told by my chain of command that I could shoot anyone who came closer to me than I felt comfortable with, if that person did not immediately move when I ordered them to do so, keeping in mind I don't speak Arabic. My chain of command's general attitude was "better them than us," and we were given guidance that reinforced that attitude across the ranks. I watched that attitude intensify throughout my three tours.

In January 2004, I remember attending a formation where we were given our mission for the second deployment. I was sitting there like a good marine with my pen and paper, and our commander told us that our mission was "to kill those who need to be killed, and save those who need to be saved." That was it. With those words, he set the tone for the deployment.

At the start of that second deployment, our standing Rules of Engagement were that someone had to be displaying hostile intent and committing a hostile act before deadly force could be used. I won't get into the absurdity of asking one to discern what is going on in the mind of another individual except to say that it was the individual marine's job to determine the meaning of hostile intent and hostile action.

During the April offensive of 2004, in which attacks erupted all over Anbar province, my unit was involved in a two-day firefight. Shortly after the firefight was underway, the same commander who had given us the mission ordered that everyone wearing a black dishdasha and a red headscarf was displaying "hostile intent" and a "hostile action" and was to be shot.

Later he ordered that *everyone* on the streets was an enemy combatant. I can remember one instance that afternoon when we came around a corner and an unarmed Iraqi man stepped out of a doorway. I remember the marine directly in front of me raising his rifle and aiming at the unarmed man. Then I think, due to some psychological reason, my brain blocked out the actual shots, because the next thing I remember is stepping over the dead man's body to clear the room that he came out of. It was a storage room and it was full of some Arabic version of Cheetos. There weren't any weapons in the area except ours.

The commander told us a couple of weeks later that over a hundred enemy "had been killed," and to the best of my knowledge that number includes the people who were shot for simply walking down the street in their own city. After the firefight was over, the standing Rules of Engagement for my unit were changed so that marines didn't need to identify a hostile action in order to use deadly force. They just had to identify hostile intent.

The rules also explicitly stated that carrying a shovel, standing on a rooftop while speaking on a cell phone, or holding binoculars or being out after curfew constituted hostile intent, and we were authorized to use deadly force.

On my third tour, the Rules of Engagement were stricter, but they only existed so that the command could say there were Rules of Engagement that were being followed. In reality, my officers explicitly told me and my fellow marines that if we felt threatened by an Iraqi's presence, we "should shoot them," and *the officers* would "take care of us."

By this time, many of the marines were on their second or third tour and had suffered such serious psychological trauma that they shot people who were clearly noncombatants. There was one incident when a roadside bomb exploded, and a few minutes later, I watched a marine start shooting at cars that were driving hundreds of meters away and in the opposite direction from where the IED exploded. We were too far away to identify who was in the cars and they didn't pose any threat to us. For all I could tell, standing about twenty meters away from the marine and about three hundred meters from the cars, they were just passing motorists. It was long enough after and far enough away from the explosion that the people in the cars might not have even known that anything had even happened, but the marine was shooting at them anyway. This marine, whose best friend had been killed on our last deployment, was also present at the two-day firefight that I mentioned earlier. He watched the commander who had given us the order to shoot anyone on the street shoot two old ladies that were walking and carrying vegetables. He said that the commander had told him to shoot the women, and when he refused, the commander shot them. So when this marine started shooting at people in cars that nobody else felt were threatening, he was following his commander's example.

In general, the Rules of Engagement changed frequently and were contradictory. When they were restrictive, they were loosely enforced. Shootings of civilians that were known were not reported because marines did not want to send their brothers-in-arms to prison when all they were trying to do was protect themselves in a situation they'd been forced into. With no way to identify their attackers, and no clear mission worth dying for, marines viewed the Rules of Engagement as either a joke or a technicality to be worked around so that they could bring each other home alive. Not only are the misuses of the Rules of Engagement in Iraq indicative of supreme strategic incompetence, they are also a moral disgrace. The people who set them should be ashamed of themselves, and they're just one of the many reasons why the troops should be withdrawn from Iraq immediately.

JASON WASHBURN

Corporal, United States Marine Corps, Rifleman

Deployments:
March 19, 2003–September 11, 2003, al-Hilla;

May 27, 2004–February 6, 2005, Najaf;

September 6, 2005–March 31, 2006, Haditha

Hometown: San Diego, California

Age at Winter Soldier: 28 years old

During the course of my three tours, the Rules of Engagement changed a lot. It seemed like every time we turned around we had different Rules of Engagement, and they told us the reasons they were changing them was because it depended on the climate of the area at the time and what the threat level was. The higher the threat the more viciously we were permitted and expected to respond.

For example, during the invasion we were told to use target identification before engaging anyone, but if the town or the city that we were approaching was a known threat, if the unit in the area before us took a high number of casualties, we were allowed to shoot whatever we wanted. It was deemed to be a free-fire zone, so we opened fire on everything, and there was really no rule governing the amount of force we were allowed to use on targets during the invasion.

I remember one woman walking by. She was carrying a huge bag, and she looked like she was heading toward us, so we lit her up with the Mark 19, which is an automatic grenade launcher, and when the dust settled, we realized that the bag was full of groceries. She had been trying to bring us food and we blew her to pieces.

After the invasion ended and Bush declared "Mission Accomplished," the rules changed pretty drastically. Instead of actually firing, we used a lot of close-combat, hand-to-hand violence to subdue people. There were a lot of times when we were on foot patrols we were ordered not to allow people to pass through our patrol formation, and unsuspecting villagers tried to pass through or cut through our formation, and we would butt-stroke them, jab them with our muzzles, or kick them just to get them out of our formations.

Another time there was a guy on a bicycle with a basketful of groceries who tried to just ride through our formation. We clothes-lined him and smashed up his bicycle. For what? Passing through our patrol formation? This is what we were expected to do.

On another mission, we were ordered to guard a fuel station. At the end of the day, when we were about to take off, a bunch of Iraqis rushed to the fuel pumps to try to take some fuel. Our squad leader called it in, and the response over the radio was, "What do you think we want you to do? Go fuck them up!" So we jumped off the trucks and charged at the Iraqis, and beat the hell out of them with rifles, fists, feet, anything we had available. Once they had either fled or were broken and bleeding, unconscious on the ground, we mounted back up in our trucks and left. We were never told to detain anyone or question anyone, just mess them up.

Most of the innocents that I actually saw get killed were behind the wheel of a vehicle, usually taxi drivers. I've been present when almost a dozen taxi drivers got killed just driving.

During my third deployment, there was a rule in place where all Iraqi traffic had to pull off of the road to let military convoys pass. If they didn't comply, or if somebody got back on the road too early, they would get shot up. If they approached a checkpoint too fast, or too recklessly, they would get shot up.

Often we were told to be on the lookout for vehicle-borne IEDs (VBIEDs)—Improvised Explosive Devices (IEDs)—matching the description of every taxi in Iraq. We were to be on the lookout for any car that has orange-paneled doors and a front that's white. That's what every taxi in Iraq looks like, and these are the cars that could be VBIEDs. Quite a few of those guys got shot up just because their car looked like the cars we were told to look out for.

In another instance, the mayor of a town near Haditha was shot. Our command gathered the whole company together, and we were shown pictures of all of this. They had pictures of what everything looked like. There was a really nice, tight shot-group in the windshield, and the command announced that this is what good marine shooting looks like, and that was the mayor of the town. It was my squad that was tasked with apologizing to the family and paying reparations. All we did was go there and give them some money and then leave. It was really a joke.

Something else we were encouraged to do, almost with a wink and nudge, was to carry drop weapons, or by my third tour, drop shovels. We would carry these weapons or shovels with us because if we accidentally shot a civilian, we could just toss the weapon on the body, and make them look like an insurgent. By my third tour, we were told that if they carried a shovel or a heavy bag, or if they were seen digging anywhere, especially near roads, that we could shoot them. So we carried these tools and weapons in our vehicles in case we accidentally shot an innocent civilian. We could just toss it on there and be like, "Well, he was digging. I was within the Rules of Engagement." This was commonly encouraged, but only behind closed doors. There obviously wasn't a public announcement, but it was pretty common. That's all I have to say.

JON MICHAEL TURNER

Lance Corporal, United States Marine Corps,
Automatic Machine-gunner, Kilo Company,
3rd Battalion, 8th Marines

Deployments:
Haiti; between Fallujah and Abu Ghraib;
March 2006, Ramadi

Hometown: Burlington, Vermont

Age at Winter Soldier: 22 years old

There's a term, once a marine, always a marine; but there's also the term, eat the apple, fuck the Corps. I don't work for you no more. [After saying that line, Turner rips off the medals he received for his service in Iraq and Haiti and threw them to the ground. Medals discarded included the Purple Heart, National Defense Service Medal, Army Expeditionary Medal, Iraq Campaign Medal, Global War on Terror Service Medal, Humanitarian Service Medal, and a Combat Action Ribbon. After doing so, he received a standing ovation from his fellow veterans.]

I want to start by showing you a video of the Executive Officer of Kilo Company. We had gotten into a two-hour long firefight, and it was over for quite some time, but he still felt the need to drop a five-hundred-pound laser-guided missile on northern Ramadi.

[Turner shows a video of the XO gloating after ordering the dropping of the bomb. In the video, the officer says:] "I think I just killed half of the population of northern Ramadi, fuck the red tape. It doesn't fucking matter."

We had gotten our Rules of Engagement brief at Camp Ramadi. Just after we had gotten that brief, our first sergeant had pulled my platoon aside and stated, "If you feel threatened in any way, shape, or form, take care of the threat, and we'll deal with it later." With that being said, "mistakes" were made on several occasions.

One incident involved an Iraqi guy we called "Mr. Wilson." My post was post Alpha, at the government center in the southwest corner. His house was directly across the street. We had a high suicide-vehicle-borne IED threat that day, and this car drove rapidly around the corner. I fired one 50-caliber machine gun round in his direction, and it ricocheted off the ground through the floorboard of the car, through his shin, and then through the roof. The car immediately came to a stop, and out of the car came seven of his daughters and Mr. Wilson himself.

A 50-caliber round is about six inches long, and the projectile is about an inch and a half long. The one shot at Mr. Wilson was a slap round, which has a polyurethane base and a titanium tip. When the projectile exits from the 50-caliber machine gun barrel, it spreads open so goes into your body leaving a hole about four inches and exits leaving you with next to nothing.

On patrol, when mistakes were made we carried "drop weapons." We took weapons from the Iraqi police during our first deployment. We took their weapons and carried them around with us, in case we messed up and shot the wrong person.

Anytime we went into a house, we took the firing pins out of their weapons. Every household is allowed to have one AK-47 for their own protection, but the weapons wouldn't fire after we took out the firing pins. Therefore, they had no protection.

[Turner shows a photo of the brain matter of an Iraqi killed by a member of his unit, sitting across the cushion of a car's front seat.] For those of you who don't know, that is brains. That was not my kill; that was one of my friends'.

When we did make mistakes, we had no respect for Iraqi bodies afterwards.

Part of an Iraqi man's face, placed on top of a Kevlar helmet for a trophy photo.

PHOTO: JON TURNER

That is a man's face on April 2, 2005, at Abu Ghraib. We sustained a very highly coordinated attack, and the next day we went ahead and had to search the premises for any remains. That face, or that part of the face, was found and put on top of a Kevlar, so a picture could be taken of it.

We had a mortar attack at Camp India, which was in between Camp Fallujah and Abu Ghraib. This was a twelve-year-old boy who was building our camp for us, and he took a piece of shrapnel to the head.

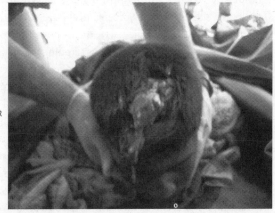

A twelve-year-old Iraqi boy took shrapnel to the head.

PHOTO: JON TURNER

On April 18, 2006, I had my first confirmed kill. He was an innocent man. I don't know his name. I call him "the Fat Man." During the incident, he walked back to his house and I shot him in front of his friend and father. The first round didn't kill him after I'd hit him in his neck. Afterwards, he started screaming and looked right into my eyes. I looked at my friend I was on post with, and I said, "Well, I can't let that happen." I took another shot and took him out. The rest of his family carried him away. It took seven Iraqis to carry his body.

We were all congratulated after we had our first kills, and that happened to have been mine. My company commander personally congratulated me. This is the same individual who stated that whoever gets their first kill by stabbing them to death would get a four-day pass when we returned from Iraq.

My third confirmed kill was a man riding his bicycle. We had Laura Logan from CBS with us, but she was with the other squad. It was later on in the day, and we went ahead and took out some individuals because we were excited about the firefight we had just gotten into. And we didn't have a cameraman or woman with us.

Anytime we did have embedded reporters with us, our actions changed drastically. We never acted the same. We were always on key with everything, did everything by the book.

House raids: Because we were a grunt battalion, we were responsible for going on several patrols. A lot of the raids and patrols we did were at night at around three o'clock in the morning. We kicked in doors and terrorized families. We segregated the women and children from the men. If the men of the household gave us problems, we'd take care of them any way we felt necessary, whether it be choking them or slapping their head against the walls.

On my wrist, there is Arabic for "fuck you." I got it put on my wrist just two weeks before we went to Iraq, because that was my choking hand and anytime I felt the need to take out aggression, I would go ahead and use it.

I'm going to show you a video of the Fatimid mosque minaret. It is riddled with bullet holes. The holes in the top of it were from mortars. A tank round went into the minaret even though we weren't sure if we were taking fire. It is illegal to shoot into a mosque unless you are taking fire from it. There was no fire that was taken from that mosque. It was shot into because we were angry. This video shows the tank round that went into the minaret.

[The video plays. A soldier inside the tank jokes over the radio:] "We are on ice cream trying to suppress the blue and white minaret.... Go ahead, take another round at that building, at that mosque over there. Another round, Kilo Two. Fuck yes. Awesome." [Video ends.]

Eighteen members of Kilo Company Third Battalion, Eighth Marines were killed in Iraq. The four crosses served as a memorial.

PHOTO: JON TURNER

There are many more stories and incidents for me to talk about although we don't have the time. Everyone sitting up here has these stories, and there's been over a million troops that have gone in and out of Iraq, so the possibilities are endless.

The reason I am doing this today is not only for myself and for the rest of society to hear. It's for all those who can't be here to talk about the things that we went through, to talk about the things that we did.

Those four crosses and this memorial service were for the five guys in Kilo Company, Third Battalion, Eighth Marines that we lost. Throughout our unit, we had eighteen that got killed.

At Winter Soldier, Jon Turner ripped off his Purple Heart and threw it to the ground.
PHOTO: MIKE HASTIE

CLIFTON HICKS

Private, United States Army, Cavalry Scout
C Troop, First Squadron, First U.S. Cavalry
Regiment

Deployment: May 2003–July 2004,
Southern Baghdad

Hometown: Gainesville, Florida

Age at Winter Soldier: 23 years old

Before I begin, I have a brief statement: For the infantrymen, scouts, and tankers of C Troop First Squadron, First United States Cavalry Regiment, there are few words which can express my admiration. I can merely say that I love them with all of my heart and that I would never have made it home alive without such worthy and courageous troopers at my side. These were men who risked everything for a cause they believed was just and true. They left behind their families, their friends, and their lives. They endured the unendurable. They did this not for greed, or jealousy, or hatred, but for the sake of love, and for that they are beyond judgment. I am no judge, and I did not come here to pass judgment either on my fellow soldiers or the officers who once commanded us in war. I'm here today to pass judgment on war itself.

First item, April 2004, free-fire zone in the Abu Ghraib neighborhood of Baghdad: During Operation Blackjack, I was instructed by our troop commander, a captain, that one sector was now a free-fire zone. He told us there were "no friendlies in the area." He said, "Game on. All weapons free."

Upon arrival in the neighborhood, the streets were littered with wreckage of vehicles. Who knows if it's a civilian vehicle or an enemy vehicle? There's no way to tell. In addition, there wasn't a single building that hadn't had a hole shot through it or something exploded inside of it. The streets were littered with human and animal corpses. I did not see military gear or weapons of any kind on any of the bodies.

I did not fire my weapon on this operation, but other members of my unit embraced the weapons-free order by firing indiscriminately into occupied civilian vehicles and at civilians themselves. They used personal weapons like rifles, vehicle-mounted weapons such as machine guns, and coaxial machine guns of various caliber. I swear until the day I die, I did not see one enemy on that operation. Judging from what I saw on the ground, the majority of those so-called KIAs were civilians attempting to flee the battlefield.

This is what happens when a conventional force such as the U.S. military attacks a heavily populated urban area. We're not bad people. We were there because we thought that we were gonna make things better, because these people wanted us to be there. We showed up and realized that there's a whole bunch of people that wanted to kill us. Guess what? They look just like the folks who don't want to kill us. How were we gonna sort them out? The only way to ensure our survival was to make sure that we put them in the dirt before they put us in the dirt, to put it bluntly.

In November 2003, an AC-130 gunship attacked a five-building apartment complex: People shot at us from these buildings. We all thought they were calling in mortar fire on our post. There were a handful of enemy fighters who tried to kill Americans out of these apartment buildings, but they were also just regular apartment buildings occupied by families. People were out on the balconies getting fresh air. There was laundry hanging off every balcony. The place was heavily populated. Besides having a handful of people with rifles who didn't really know how to shoot them and a handful of people who spotted for mortars, it was packed full of innocent families and it was in no way a legitimate military target.

But one day the squadron commander, who was a lieutenant colonel, rode by in his personal Humvee and they shot at him. So the command went around and told everybody that at ten o'clock that night they were gonna put on a show for us. So this AC-130 showed up and didn't just strafe or shoot a few rounds here and there; it approached and launched sustained attack on those buildings.

I don't recall exactly how long it circled. These planes circle until they expend their ammunition. The main weapon they used in this raid was the 40mm cannon, which loads automatically and can fire a round every half second or so. The 40mm round is like a hand grenade, and it fired maybe a hundred rounds.

On January 21, 2004—I have the exact dates because I wrote about all this in my journal—a civilian was run over by one of our Humvees and left for dead. We had been on a long night mission. We had been out all night and were tired, wanted to go home and hit the rack. There had been a lot of shooting that night. It had been a real bad night and we just wanted it to be over. We wanted to go home.

The guys ahead of us arrived at the gate when they apparently ran somebody over. I knew the guys in that Humvee. The driver's one of my best friends, and the staff sergeant in command was also a very close friend. Later he was killed over there. The staff sergeant ordered the driver to continue driving and then ordered everyone on patrol not to say anything about it. He did this not because he was afraid of getting in trouble for killing somebody, but because he didn't want to have to wait around and fill out a report. He didn't want to be inconvenienced. They just wanted to go home and go to sleep.

As I said in my opening statement, these troopers are not bad people. These are people like any of us, but when put in terrible situations they respond horribly. When you are around that much death, running over some guy who was standing in the road is not a big deal. What's a big deal is being separated from your cot another two or three hours, having to talk about it.

So they didn't say anything, and we rolled up on them. We were the idiots who stopped and called it up and we got stuck out there for three hours, and after that, we made sure that if we saw anybody dead or anything like that we just kept going because it wasn't worth the trouble.

February 21, 2004—civilians killed and wounded by American small arms fire.

It was during another nighttime patrol. This was an unusually friendly neighborhood, where people came out and waved. People didn't seem to hate us. We were riding around and we heard an IED blast up ahead and AK-47 fire. Then we heard M-16s firing back, which are our rifles. We could tell that some of our people were in a fight. We raced ahead, eager to get some of the action, but by the time we showed up, the fight was over.

So there was the patrol of 82nd Airborne guys, infantry guys, and Humvees and they were packed in these unarmored fiberglass Humvees with machine guns pointing out on either side. They were attacked by two or three insurgents. They were in an open field, laying in a ditch across on their left. On their right was a civilian neighborhood, with housing for disabled military families from the Iraqi army.

The Airborne guys had taken fire from the left. Some of the guys also had heard gunfire coming in from the right, so the whole platoon returned fire in both directions. When the firing stopped, they sent some guys who ran out into the field. They didn't find any insurgents. They looked for blood trails, didn't find any blood trails. They didn't find anything but some empty shell casings. The rest of them immediately dismounted and kicked in the door of this house that they had taken fire from. They were gonna raid the house and maybe catch the guy who had been shooting at them.

When they kicked in the door of this house, what they found was an entire extended Iraqi family celebrating a wedding. For those of us who have been in Iraq or at least in Baghdad, you know that any excuse they have is a good excuse to get on the roof and shoot their guns in the air. It's a celebratory thing. We've all heard of celebratory fire being mistaken for hostile fire and this is a textbook case of that. Old Grandpa was on top of the roof cuttin' loose with his rifle because he was so happy that his daughter was getting married. Meanwhile this 82nd patrol in his front yard gets ambushed from across the road and they returned fire in both directions.

They hit three people inside the wedding party. One was an adult man, who was slightly wounded, another young girl of maybe ten was slightly wounded. But there was another girl who was six or seven and she was dead. I was in the gunner's hatch of the Humvee. I didn't get out and go inside the house, but I looked through the doorway and that was the first time that I had ever seen a six-year-old girl dead.

This happens every day. People always say, "Yeah, well, that's war," and that *is* war, and that's especially this war. Little girls get killed by soldiers in Iraq every day, not because we want to, but just because it happens. What happened next was that the 82nd patrol just mounted up and left it with us. It was our responsibility. Once again, we got stuck calling this up. We called it up to our Tactical Operations Center, and we told them what happened. They told us to continue mission. They said, "Charlie Mike" and that's military jargon for continue mission.

So we hopped up in our Humvees and rode out. We didn't even have a translator and we didn't speak Arabic. We couldn't say "sorry." We just hopped in our vehicle and rode off.

For obvious reasons, it's difficult to get up here and talk about these things. But what's also difficult is that right after this happened, we never talked about it again. We drove away. We didn't even tell the other guys back at the post about this. This was something that we just stuffed it the back in our minds and we thought, "Well, these things happen." It was just forgotten and then the occupation dragged on.

STEVEN CASEY

Specialist, United States Army, Cavalry Scout
Deployment: April 2003–July 2004, Baghdad and the surrounding areas
Hometown: Farmington, Missouri
Age at Winter Soldier: 24 years old

I was in the same unit as Clif. During the November 2003 free-fire zone Clif was talking about, our Lieutenant Colonel Chuck Williams's personal Humvee had been purportedly shot at. He did an interview with CBS the afternoon before the incident.

He said, "If you are trying to send a message by firing and harboring yourself inside of an area like this, we want to send the message right back that you can be reached. We will find you and surgically remove you."

Spectre Gunships are not a precision weapon. There's no precision to it as there is with surgery, so to have him use that comparison is a little odd. I have video footage of the air strike itself, and the most disturbing part was the parties on the rooftops. Our roofs were set up in a semicircle around this post, and in building after building everyone was told to grab their chairs and popcorn and jerky and go on top and watch this thing go down. I was there. I probably hooped and hollered as well. There are higher-up NCOs on the video saying, "Can you hear haji die?" "We don't have zone five anymore because they just blew the shit out of it." And lots of cheering. You know there are civilians there, but that's what we're supposed to do.

I never got a true body count out of it. We never went to inspect the rubble afterwards, but I can tell you that it happened. Clif can tell you that it happened. He was in a separate building at a different vantage point watching the same show.

Another one of their main objectives was to rid the camp of the mortar, but the mortar fire continued almost every day even after this target was destroyed, so he may have done some surgery or what have you, but I can assure you that I still have plenty of issues with loud noises caused by the mortars landing daily on and around my post, and I just don't see any justification for it all.

I was in the forward platoon doing operations on the streets. There were no friendlies. In April of 2004 we were scheduled to go home, but due to a rise in violence we had to remain and we returned to the Operation Blackjack. We went to the city of Abu Ghraib, where we were supposed to secure and patrol.

Several buildings had already been bulldozed by American engineering companies, two had been flattened. Rubble and vehicles were piled up on the side of the road and set ablaze. That's how they cleaned up the area and weeded out the bad guys. We were a cleanup crew after that, and we witnessed several different instances where people took advantage of the free-fire order.

I witnessed personal weapons being fired into the radiators and windshields because these vehicles were coming up the correct side of the road that we were going down the wrong way. Our orders at this point in time were to have one vehicle on each side of the highway and ensure there was no one on the highway besides us.

There's only so much hand-waving you can really do from a vehicle, and those who didn't turn around, unfortunately, were neutralized one way or another. I personally witnessed shots fired into windshields and radiators well over twenty different times. I personally never fired at these and used the free-fire order, but there was a lot of collateral damage. No combatant damage that I can recall at that point in time by the people I was with.

Lastly, I want to talk about the way the raids were conducted. Usually what we found, what happened in raids is what the military calls a "dry hole" or "whoops." This happened several times.

There was one raid, just a typical night raid. It was my platoon and a couple of Bradleys. We rolled out to this house. Typically there were concrete walls around the house, with closed and secured metal gates. So we would pivot and steer the Bradleys into the walls to knock down the wall and tear down whatever security infrastructure the person's home had. Sometimes we would even crush the vehicles parked behind the wall. After doing that, we dropped a ramp and continued inside.

Then we started hearing a lady screaming from the inside, her and her children. We get to the door and bust the door in, and take her and her children to what we call the EPW roundup area, which is where a couple of lower-enlisted soldiers would take the enemy prisoners of war, like this lady and her children, at gunpoint and hold them until the raid was complete. Next, we entered their house and destroyed it. We rummaged through her personal effects looking for weapons. We punctured the walls looking for soft spots. We'd heard the insurgents were putting things in the walls, so that was our order.

To make this long story short, we destroyed this lady's house and we found nothing. We've scared her and her children to death and come to find out we were off by a number. We were supposed to raid the house across the street. I actually said, "Hey, we've got time. Why don't we go?" However, we didn't go. We chalked it up, and as Clif says, "Charlie Mike." We went home and maybe went to bed.

This was not an isolated incident for my platoon. I can't blame the people who did it. I was one of them. We were all good people. We were just in a bad situation and we did what we had to do to get through. So for all those in the video and that I served with, like Clifton, I have to thank them, and I hope they hear it.

JESSE HAMILTON
Staff Sergeant, United States Army Reserve,
Fire Support Specialist
Deployment: July 2005–July 2006, Fallujah
Hometown: Philadelphia, Pennsylvania
Age at Winter Soldier: 28 years old

I worked as part of a ten-man team while I was in Iraq, so I didn't serve with a lot of different U.S. soldiers and marines over there. I did work with a lot of the Iraqi forces though, and if you want my opinion as to whether or not Rules of Engagement actually exist within the Iraqi army, the answer is no.

We had some phrases: "Spray 'n pray," where the Iraqis would just start shooting and pray they hit the enemy, if there was one. "The death blossom" was also a term we used regularly, because once the shooting started, death would blossom all around.

I never saw any civilians get killed by these actions, but one instance sticks out in my mind. I lived in Fallujah the whole time that I was in Iraq, on an Iraqi firm base, and the enemy would take potshots at us. They would shoot RPGs at us. We'd get mortared and as soon as something like that would happen, the Iraqi guards on the roof would start a barrage of fire. It didn't matter where the fire had initially come from, if it was just mortars or a combination. They would just start shooting. One day I ran up to the roof. And while I couldn't see any incoming fire, I saw the Iraqis shooting indiscriminately, and that was normal. I saw a civilian running and the wall that she was running in front of was just peppered by bullets. The Iraqis weren't shooting *at* her. I know that for a fact. They weren't aiming at her. They were just shooting indiscriminately.

Iraqis can be very brutal. We would often take in prisoners. Sometimes it wouldn't even be on a joint mission. The Iraqis would conduct presence patrols and bring people in for questioning. They weren't overly nice, but they weren't overly brutal in those situations. But when we took Iraqi casualties, that's really when the tides turned. I saw Iraqi soldiers make prisoners run the gauntlet from the vehicle in which they were transported to the S2 Intelligence Office where they would be questioned. Our job as American advisers was to try our best to stop that, and we did. However, there's only so much you can do, and you can't prevent it all. We weren't there when prisoners initially got picked up. More times than not, the guys that they were bringing in got released after a short questioning.

After a while I was almost like, "I don't care. I'm over it." I tried to stop it, but I just stopped caring. It was their people and that's what they were gonna do. We're just ordinary people that decided to pick up a uniform and serve this nation and you can only take so much. We're sons, we're brothers. Some are fathers. When people take pot shots at you, shoot RPGs at your house, mortar you, it begins to wear on your mind and that creates apathy.

The Iraqis have been doing their thing for thousands of years and I think it is very pretentious of us as Americans to think that we can go in there and spoon-feed them democracy. I think it's even more pretentious to try to go in there and change their culture and the way they handle situations. I think that it is a lost cause in Iraq. I think that regardless of when we leave, whether it is tomorrow or in a hundred years, the Iraqis are going to handle things the way that they're going to handle them. It's their culture. It's their country. We are allegedly giving them democracy, so let's give it to them and let's let them do what they want with their country and their lives.

At this point, given my experience working, living, speaking in Arabic with my Iraqi counterparts, getting to know them and getting to care about them, and with my military history and my friends who are in the U.S. military, I don't think that it's worth it to continue losing American lives, to continue what we now see in hindsight as a pretty big mistake. I just don't think it's worth it.

JASON HURD

Specialist, Tennessee National Guard, Medic Troop F, 2nd Squadron 278th Regimental Combat Team

Deployment: November 2004–November 2005, Central Baghdad

Hometown: Kingsport, Tennessee

Age at Winter Soldier: 28 years old

I'm from a little place nestled in the mountains of east Tennessee called Kingsport and hence the mountain-man beard. People don't really trust you if you're clean-shaven there. Kingsport is truly small-town America. There's a Baptist church on every street corner and even the high-class restaurants serve biscuits and gravy. My father, Carl C. Hurd, who died in 2000 at seventy-six years old, was a marine during World War II. Shortly after he died, I had the two World War II battles he participated in tattooed on my arm, because my father had the same tattoo. He was in the Pacific Campaign and participated in the Battles of Tarawa and Guadalcanal, which were some of the bloodiest occurrences of that war.

I decided to join the military in 1997. I was seventeen years old. I had just graduated from high school and I didn't know exactly what I wanted to do with my life. My father was adamantly opposed to me serving in the military. My father was one of the most war-mongering, gun-loving people you could ever meet, but he didn't feel that way when it came to his son because he knew the negative psychological consequence of combat service. Looking back, I know for a fact that my father had Post-Traumatic Stress Disorder. He had the rage, he had the nightmares, and he had the flashbacks.

I decided against my father's wishes to go into the military as a medic in August of 1997. Originally, I intended to do my four years and get off of active-duty and go to college in Johnson City, Tennessee. But about a month before I left active duty, a National Guard recruiter approached me and said, "Hey we've got an expanded unit in your hometown in Kingsport and if you decide to join that, we can give you a lot of college money." And he offered me so much college money I decided to sign up for six more years in the Tennessee National Guard.

I got into Iraq in November of '04 and I was there until November of '05. Our first six months in country were relatively uneventful. After a few months, we moved on to another mission, patrolling the Kindi Street area, right outside the Green Zone. Kindi Street is a relatively upscale neighborhood, and some of the houses would cost well over a million dollars here in America. From what we were told, this area had no violent activity at all up until the point that we started patrolling there. We were the first U.S. military to do so on any regular basis. So we went in and we started doing patrols through the streets. We started meeting and greeting the local population, trying to figure out what sort of issues they had and how we could resolve them.

We were out on a dismounted patrol one day, walking by a woman's house. She was outside working in her garden. Our interpreter threw up his hand and said, "Salam Alaikum," which means "Peace of God be with you." She said. "No. No peace of God be with you." She was angry and so we stopped and our interpreter said, "Well, what's the matter? Why are you so angry? We're here to ensure your safety." That woman began to tell us a story.

Just a few months prior, her husband had been shot and killed by a United States convoy because he got too close to their convoy. He was not an insurgent. He was not a terrorist. He was a working man trying to make a living for his family.

To make matters worse, a Special Forces team operating in the Kindi area holed up in a building there and made a compound out of it. A few weeks after this man died, the Special Forces team got some intelligence that this woman was supporting the insurgency, so they raided her home, zip-tied her and her two children, threw them on the floor, and detained her son and took him away. For the next two weeks, this woman had no idea whether her son was alive, dead, or worse. At the end of that two weeks, the Special Forces team rolled up, dropped her son off, and without so much as an apology drove off. It turns out they had acted on bad intelligence.

Things like that happen every day in Iraq. We are harassing these people. We are disrupting their lives.

One day we were on another dismounted patrol through the Kindi

Street area. We were walking past an area we called the Garden Center because it was literally a fenced-off garden. As is policy, we kept all cars and
individuals away from our formation. So a car was approaching us from
the front. I was at the rear of the formation because I was the medic and the
medics hang out at the back with the platoon sergeant in case anything
happens up front so you can respond.

They waved the car off down a side street so that it would not come near
our formation. As I made it to the side street, the car turned around and
was coming back toward us because the street was blocked off by a concrete T barrier. I began doing my levels of aggression. I held up my hand
trying to get the car to stop. The car sped up and I thought to myself, "Oh
my God, this is it. This is someone who is trying to hurt us."

So instead of doing what I should have done according to policy and
raising my weapon, instead I did what you should never do and I took my
hands off of my weapon altogether and began jumping up and down waving my hands back and forth trying to get this car to stop and see me. The
car kept coming and so I raised my weapon and the car kept coming. I
pulled my selector switch off of safe and the car kept coming. I was applying pressure to my trigger, getting ready to fire on the vehicle and out of
nowhere a man came off the side of the road, flagged the car down, and got
it to pull over. He opened the driver's side door, and out popped an eighty-
year-old woman. This woman was a highly respected figure in the community and I don't have a clue what would have happened had I opened fire
on her. I would imagine a riot.

To this day, that is the worst thing that I have ever done in my life. I am
a peaceful person, but yet in Iraq I drew down on an eighty-year-old geri-
atric woman who could not see me because I was in front of a desert-colored building wearing desert-colored camouflage.

The next mission we got was to man the main checkpoint that entered
into the Green Zone. We called this checkpoint Slaughterhouse 11, because
a car bomb goes off almost every single morning at checkpoint 11. The first
day we took over that checkpoint, a car bomb drove into it and exploded.
My guys were able to find cover and it didn't hurt them, but it killed and injured untold numbers of Iraqi civilians in queue for the checkpoint. I
treated five people that day, and I imagine twenty or thirty others got carted
off in civilian ambulances before I could get to them. I remember a man

running toward me carrying a young seventeen- or eighteen-year old Iraqi guy, very thin, and very pale. The guy was missing parts of his arm; his arm and his forearm were only held on by a small flap of skin. The bones were protruding and he was bleeding profusely. He had shrapnel wounds all over his torso and his entire left butt cheek was missing and it was bleeding profusely, and it was pooling blood.

To this day I have that image burned in my mind's eye. Every couple of days I get a flash of red color in my mind's eye and it won't have any shape, no form, just a flash of red and every time I associate it with that instance. Not only are we disrupting the lives of Iraqi civilians, we are disrupting the lives of our veterans.

Conservative statistics say that the majority of Iraqis support attacks against coalition forces. The majority of Iraqis support us leaving immediately and the majority of Iraqis see us as the main contributors to the violence in Iraq.

I like to explain it this way, especially in the South because it rings with truth to people down there: If a foreign occupying force came here to the United States, whether they told us they were here to liberate us or to give us democracy, do you not think that every person that owns a shotgun would not come out of the hills and fight for their right to self-determination? Another time I was out on patrol in the Kindi Street area. I approached a man with my interpreter on the side of the road and said, "Look, are your lives better because we are here? Are you safer? Do you feel more secure? Do you feel like we are liberating you?" That man looked me straight in the eye and said, "Mister, we Iraqis know that you have good intentions here, but the fact is that before America invaded, we didn't have to worry about car bombs in our neighborhoods. We didn't have to worry about the safety of our own children before they walked to school, and we didn't have to worry about U.S. soldiers shooting at us as we drive up and down our own streets."

Ladies and gentlemen, the suffering in Iraq is tearing that country apart. Ending that suffering begins with a complete and immediate withdrawal of all of our troops.

ADAM KOKESH

Sergeant, United States Marine Corps Reserve, Civil Affairs

Deployment: February 18–September 14, 2004, Fallujah

Hometown: Claremont, California

Age at Winter Soldier: 26 years old

I was against the war before the war. Even though I believed all of the lies that Colin Powell told at the UN, all the intelligence, all the spin. I didn't think it was going to be worth it, but in 2004 I thought that we were cleaning up our mess and genuinely trying to do good by the Iraqi people. That was something I wanted to be a part of, and something that I enthusiastically risked my life for.

This is the Rules of Engagement card that I was issued for our deployment to Iraq [Kokesh holds up his U.S. Marine Corps Rules of Engagement card, which is reproduced in the appendix of this volume.]

This is held up as the gold standard of conduct in the occupation right now, and they couldn't even cut it square. I'll read a part of it. It says, "Nothing on this card prevents you from using deadly force to defend yourself. Enemy, military, and paramilitary forces may be attacked, subject to the following instructions: Positive identification is required prior to engagement. Positive identification is 'reasonable certainty'"–that's in quotes on the card—"that your target is a legitimate military target." We were supposed to keep this in our breast pocket.

In April of 2004, we got an order to pack for three days and have our vehicle and a convoy ready to go at midnight. We weren't told where we were going. This was right after the four Blackwater security agents were killed and had their bodies burned and hung from the northern bridge over the Euphrates on the western side of Fallujah.

During the siege of Fallujah, we changed Rules of Engagement more often than we changed our underwear. At first it was, "You follow the Rules of Engagement. You do what you're supposed to do." Then there were times when it was, "You can shoot any suspicious observer." So someone with binoculars and a cell phone was fair game, and that opened things up to a lot of subjectivity.

At one point we imposed a curfew on Fallujah, and then we were allowed to shoot anything after dark. Fortunately, I was never forced to make that decision, but there were a lot of marines who were forced to make that choice.

In one incident, in the first couple of days we were there, there was a checkpoint shooting to the west of our perimeter. We were told a vehicle was approaching an impromptu vehicle checkpoint at a high rate of speed. That gave marines manning the checkpoint cause to be suspicious and they unloaded into that vehicle with a .50-caliber machine gun. The idea is that anybody coming at your position who doesn't slow down to five miles an hour is an enemy combatant. Well, this is at dusk and marines are all wearing camouflage and this guy could just have been cruising through his neighborhood, or rushing home to see his family. We didn't know, but it was enough that the marines got jumpy and shot a burst of .50-cal rounds into this vehicle.

The bullets started at the bumper and went up the engine compartment and then one round at least hit this Iraqi in the chest so hard that it broke his chair backwards and we saw the vehicle burning in the distance. Everybody tried to justify it and say, oh, they heard rounds cooking off in the fire, AK-47 rounds were bursting in the trunk or somewhere in the car. The next day they dragged the car into our sleeping area, and it was clear that there were no holes from rounds cooking off in the side of this car.

Kokesh poses for a trophy photo with a dead Iraqi outside Fallujah in the spring of 2004.

PHOTO: ADAM KOKESH

I posed on the hood of that car, and as someone mentioned earlier, it felt funny not because what we were doing was morally wrong, but because I wasn't the one that killed this guy. There was a group of us marines that all took turns taking pictures and posing like this. At the first Winter Soldier in 1971, one of the testifiers showed a similar picture and said, "Don't ever let your government do this to you." Our government is still doing this to patriotic young men and women who have volunteered their lives in the service of this country, putting them in a situation where this kind of thing is normal.

At one point during the siege of Fallujah we decided to let women and children out of the city. We thought it was the most gracious thing we could have done. I went out on the northern bridge over the Euphrates on the western side of Fallujah, and our guidelines were that males had to be under fourteen years old. If they were old enough to be in your fighting hole, they were too old to get out of the city. I had to go there and turn these men back.

We thought that we were doing something really noble and gracious, and it took me a long time before I could think about what a horrible decision we were forcing these families to make. They could split up and leave their husband and older sons in the city and hope a Spectre gunship round doesn't land on their head, or stay with them and hunker down and just hope that they made it through alive.

After the siege of Fallujah, my civil affairs team was pulled to set up a Civil Military Operations Center or CMOC two clicks east of Fallujah. My role there was manning the front checkpoint. We didn't have enough translators and I was learning Arabic and spoke enough to run a checkpoint without a translator. We were still putting down Spectre gunship rounds into the city, and one night some of those rounds started a fire. Iraqi firefighters and policemen responded and they were silhouetted against the fire. Since the marine's Rules of Engagement at that time were to shoot anything after dark, marines started firing at these firefighters and policemen.

An Iraqi policeman woke me up in the middle of the night and through pointing, pantomime, the little Arabic I spoke at the time, and a translation dictionary, I was able to figure out that marines were shooting at Iraqi firefighters and cops. We sent it down our chain of command and stopped it from happening, but how many incidents like that happen? I know that that happened while I was there, during the siege of Fallujah.

One day in the middle of summer I got a random call on my field phone at the checkpoint saying, "Take one marine and get up to the road and stop any black Opel that comes your way," because al-Qaeda in Iraq leader Abu Musab al-Zarqawi was fleeing the city in a black Opel. All I could say was, "What's an Opel?"

I got up there, and I was with my marine, he was behind me, and I saw a black blur coming toward us, and I was like, "Hey, is that a black Opel?" He was like, "That's a black blur, Sergeant."

So I got up on the road and I pointed my rifle down the freeway—the main road between Fallujah and Baghdad. I yelled, "Kif! Stop!" at this car that's going about fifty miles an hour. It whizzed right by me and I turned around, and was like, "Oh, crap, I hope I don't have to shoot out his tires." Fortunately he stopped and I pulled him out. The other marine was right behind me. We got there, we pulled him out of the car and said, "We need to search you." They hadn't told me that I was looking for Zarqawi, so I was like, "Alright, get out of the car." He had his wife and his kids in the back seat. I frisked him and called up and said, "Got one 'pak' detained. Please advise. Over."

My staff sergeant came out, trotted up, after coming out of the air-conditioned building, and he pulls out the al-Zarqawi "wanted" poster. He looks at the person we had stopped and then he looks at the poster and goes, "Ah, that's not him. Let him go." That kind of thing, where we're just harassing people unnecessarily, is part of daily life.

A lot of people who were detained are innocent. There are a lot of people who get detained who are guilty, but guilty or innocent, they usually get similar treatment. Even at Abu Ghraib, they'll do six months and get out because we don't have the capacity to provide any kind of due process.

We're really pissing a lot of people off that way. If the game for the insurgency is: shoot at Americans and if you get caught, if you're not killed, you'll do six months and you'll get out, then—not that being at Abu Ghraib is a picnic by any means—but the game is understood.

When I was activated, we were told we'd be working on schools and mosques and clinics and water projects, and rebuilding Iraq. I was really excited about that. I thought we were going to be the tip of the spear, and we were going to be leading the charge to rebuild Iraq.

We were six-man teams attached to these larger infantry units: regiments or battalions, usually. You couldn't go anywhere in Fallujah without six Humvees and machine guns, and we were just six marines. So we had to beg these infantry commanders to tag along on their convoys so we could do our missions. We were constantly struggling to justify our existence, and we came up with a slogan: "We care so that you don't have to." To the macabre Marine Corps sense of humor that's pretty funny. But it's easy to step back and think, "Man, we've got units in Iraq whose job is to care so that someone else doesn't have to. But that someone else isn't just those grunts in infantry, but it was everybody all the way up." We care so that Paul Bremer doesn't have to, so that the chiefs of staff don't have to, so that Congress doesn't have to, and so that the president can gush on and on about how much he cares about the Iraqi people while continuing a policy that is decimating their country.

And we care so the American people don't have to, so that these things can go on in our names and they can just go back to the mall and their daily lives and pretend like nothing's wrong. That's one of the things that disturbs me the most about the state of affairs right now.

VINCENT EMANUELE

Private First Class, United States Marine Corps, Rifleman

Deployments: March 2003–May 2003, from Kuwait to Iraq;

August 2004–April 2005, al-Qaim

Hometown: Chesterton, Indiana

Age at Winter Soldier: 23 years old

An act that took place quite often in Iraq was taking pot shots at cars that drove by. This was quite easy for most marines to get away with because our Rules of Engagement stated that the town of al-Qaim had already been forewarned and knew to pull their cars to a complete stop when approaching a United States convoy. Of course, the consequences of such actions pose a huge problem for those of us who patrol the streets every day. This was not the best way to become friendlier with an already hostile local population. This was not an isolated incident, and it took place for most of our eight-month deployment.

We were sent out on a mission to blow up a bridge that was supposedly being used to transport weapons across the Euphrates, and we were ambushed. We were forced to return fire in order to make our way out of the city. This incident took place in the middle of the day, and most of those who were engaging us were not in clear view. Many hid in local houses and businesses and were part of the local population themselves, once again making it very hard to determine who was shooting from where and where exactly to return fire. This led to our squad shooting at everything and anything, i.e., properties, cars, people, in order to push through the town. I fired most of my magazines into the town, but not once did I clearly identify the targets that I was shooting at.

Once we were taking rocket fire from a town and a member of our squad mistakenly identified a tire shop as being the place where the rocket fire came from. Sure enough, we mortared the shop. This was one of the only times we actually had the chance to investigate what we had done and to talk to the people we had directly affected. Luckily, the family who owned the shop was still alive. However, we were not able to compensate the family, nor were we able to explain how it was he could rebuild his livelihood. This was not an isolated incident, and it took place over the course of our eight-month deployment.

Another task our platoon took on was transporting prisoners from our base back to the desert. The reason I say the desert and not their town is because that is exactly where we would drop them off, in the middle of nowhere. Now, most of these men had obviously been deemed innocent, or else they would have been moved to a more permanent prison and not released back into the population. We took it upon ourselves to punch, kick, butt-stroke, or generally harass these prisoners. Then, we would take them to the middle of the desert, throw them out of the back of our Humvees while continually kicking, punching, and at times throwing softball-sized rocks at their backs as they ran away from our convoy. Once again, this is not an isolated incident, and this took place over the duration of our eight-month deployment.

The last and possibly the most disturbing of what took place in Iraq was the mishandling of the dead. On several occasions, our convoy came across bodies that had been decapitated and were lying on the side of the road. When encountering these bodies, standard procedure was to run over the corpses, sometimes even stopping and taking pictures with these bodies,

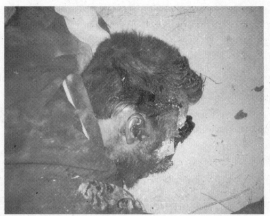

A man shot in the head by Vincent Emanuele lay in a ditch for at least two weeks after he was killed. This photo became the screen-saver on the laptop belonging to "one of our more motivated marines."

PHOTO: VINCENT EMANUELE

which was also standard practice whenever we encountered the dead. On one specific occasion, I had shot a man in the back of the head after we saw him planting an IED device; we pulled his body out of the ditch he was laying in and left it to rot in the field. We saw the body again up to two weeks later. There were also pictures taken of this gentleman, and his picture became the screen-saver on the laptop belonging to one of our more motivated marines.

The larger point that I'd like to touch on is that these are the consequences for sending young men and women into battle. These are the things that happen. And what I'd like to ask anyone who's viewing this testimony is to imagine your loved ones put in such positions. Your brothers, your sisters, your nieces, your nephews, your aunts, and your uncles, and more importantly, and maybe most importantly, to be able to put ourselves in the Iraqis' shoes who encountered these events every day and for the last five years.

SERGIO KOCHERGIN

Corporal, United States Marine Corps, Rifleman
First Battalion Seventh Marines Scouts Sniper Platoon

Deployments: February 2, 2003–October 2, 2003, from Kuwait to Baghdad;

August 27, 2004–March 20, 2005, along the Syrian border

Hometown: Eugene, Oregon

Age at Winter Soldier: 23 years old

O ur area of operation was near Vincent Emanuele's, along the Syrian border. It was a little base. The town was not secure when we arrived, and the initial Rules of Engagement were if a person had a weapon, or there's suspicious activity going on, we had to call the commanding post, request permission, assess the situation, and see what we were going to do.

The third day after we arrived, our company commander, our first lieutenant, and one of our NCOs all got killed by an IED. As time went on, and as the casualties grew in number, the Rules became lenient. Because we saw our friends getting blown up and killed every day, we didn't really question them. We were angry. We just wanted to do our job and come back

We used "drop weapons." Drop weapons are the weapons that were given to us by our chain of command in case we killed somebody without weapons so that we would not get into trouble. We would carry an AK-47 and if the person that was shot did not have the weapon, the AK-47 would be placed at his corpse. Then, when the unit would come back to the base they would turn it in to identify the shot man as an enemy combatant. The weapons could not come from anyone else but the higher chain of command because after a raid all the weapons are turned into the armory and should be recorded.

The Rules of Engagement were very flexible. After our own casualties mounted the Rules changed. We were allowed to engage anyone with a weapon without calling in and asking permission from the higher command. Two months into the deployment our Rules were to engage any personnel with a heavy bag and a shovel at the intersections or on the roads. This gave us a bigger window on who we can engage. Looking at the situation from this point of view a lot of the enemy combatants that we shot were really civilians in the wrong place at the wrong time.

One of our intelligence officers told us that they received a call from one of the sources in the city, telling them that there were flyers posted all over the town that said that there were unknown snipers in the city that kill the insurgents and the civilians. We did not take into consideration that these innocent people were being killed by us, because every time we sent the pictures to the command post through an interlink system, we would receive an approval to kill people with shovels and heavy bags. Now I know that it was not right to do that, but when you trust those who act like they care for you, you listen to them and follow their orders because you don't want to let your friends down. "What if...?" was used as propaganda and a way to relieve our minds from the actions we have partaken in and make it easier on us.

Finally, I want to tell you is about a roommate who we shared the bathroom with back in the United States. He was on the suicide watch for a few months on and off. The last three weeks before we deployed he was constantly on the watch. A week before a family day he was released from the watch so that he would not say anything to his parents and he did not say anything to them. About a month into the deployment he blew his brains out in one of the shower stalls. Actions like that show the poor judgment of our command who don't care for the troops just to save their own skin. That marine should have not gone to Iraq in the first place and nobody was held responsible for his death. If they do not care for their own marines what care do they have for the people of Iraq when they give the orders?

I want to apologize to all the people in Iraq. I'm sorry, and I hope this is going to be over as soon as possible.

LOGAN LAITURI

Sergeant, United States Army, Medic/Forward Observer, 114 Golden Dragons Second Brigade 25th Infantry Division

Deployments: January 19, 2004–February 15, 2005, Quick Reaction Force

Hometown: Camden, New Jersey

Age at Winter Soldier: 26 years old

My unit moved around a lot. The Rules of Engagement would change. First of all, they were mostly verbal. We never were given ROE cards. When Adam Kokesh flashed one in front of everybody this morning, that was the first time I saw one. I didn't think they existed. So we never got any concrete ROE that defined our missions, and what our levels of aggression were allowed to be. We were told there were five S's: Signal, shout, show, shove, shoot, and that was our ROE.

The golden rule, the one that we could always count on, was that if you feel threatened, don't hesitate to use your weapon if you feel it's necessary. If something occurred, we could always say that we were threatened, and I observed that a couple of times with other members of my unit.

I experienced a very permissive ROE in Najaf around July 2004. Rolling into the city, Muqtada al-Sadr was our enemy at that time, and we were told anybody in black clothing with a green headband is fair game to shoot. It was made very clear that this is the uniform of the enemy, and we should take them out whenever necessary. I think that was the closest we got to conventional warfare, for which I trained for five years before I went to Iraq.

In Samara in October 2004, I was a part of Operation Baton Rouge. We were the first light infantry to enter the city of Samara from the west. It was a train-up for Fallujah. We were told it was a litmus test to see what procedures we would need to incorporate into the attack on Fallujah in November.

Going into Samara, we were told that all of the civilians knew we were coming. They were supposed to stay in their house or evacuate. The following day one of the snipers saw a man crossing the street with a bag in his hand and shot him. The fact that this was within the ROE doesn't satisfy my ethical restrictions.

The turning point in the war for me came on November 16 in 2004 in Joiga. I was on a rocket man patrol. We were looking for mortar men. We got a call to assist another unit that had had an accident on the convoy. A vehicle had overturned over a reservoir. The overturned vehicle was resting partly over the water and partly land.

I was asked to get in the water and look for bodies, which I did. About an hour into it, after I had gotten out of the water, I was circling the vehicle looking for things to do when I saw a set of legs sticking out from what used to be the door to the Humvee. At first glance, I thought it was a rescuer talking to someone pinned by the vehicle to whom we had already given morphine. I tapped him on the leg. I didn't get a response.

I indicated to one of the medics I thought this was a casualty and that he needed attention. The medic responded that he was too far gone and we need to focus on the people who have a chance. So for an hour and a half, I fretted about what to do about this guy. Combat triage is the opposite from triage in a hospital where you rush the most immediate to the operating room. In combat, if someone doesn't have a chance, you make it as comfortable for them as possible to die.

Finally, a crane came, lifted the vehicle, got the guy out that was pinned by his leg who had morphine already injected into him. The Special Forces medics got the other guy up and he had a pulse, he was still alive. I heard on the radio going back to Kirkuk that he had died before he could reach the clinic, and for some reason that hit me pretty hard.

For nine nights I didn't sleep. I realized that there's a great possibility that he had died hearing everybody around him and knowing that nobody was coming to his aid. In the tents at night, in the pitch dark, I couldn't stop thinking about how it felt being trapped under a Humvee and possibly not being able to catch a breath and cry for help. And then I realized that, despite all the Iraqi bodies I had seen throughout Iraq, it was an American soldier that made me disturbed. I still wrestle with that. What does that mean? That I saw these dead Iraqis, but it took an American soldier, someone my own race and creed and skin color, to wake me up out of slumber.

I wanted to close with why I do this. Martin Luther King said of the war in Vietnam, and I would apply it to the War on Terror: "…I oppose the war in Vietnam, because I love America. I speak out against this war, not in anger, but with anxiety and sorrow in my heart…:. I speak out against this war because I am disappointed with America. And there can be no great disappointment where there is no great love. I am disappointed with our failure to deal positively and forthrightly with the triple evils of racism, economic exploitation, and militarism. We are presently moving down a dead-end road that can lead to national disaster." And I don't want a national disaster.

HART VIGES

Specialist, United States Army, Infantry, 82nd Airborne Division, First 325HHC, Battalion Mortars

Deployment: February 2003–February 2004, Samawa, Fallujah, Baghdad

Hometown: Kirkland, Washington; Austin, Texas

Age at Winter Soldier: 32 years old

We were set up outside the town of Samawa in a garbage dump. Flies were so heavy we couldn't eat. When the sun was up, we'd eat a mouthful of flies with our MRE pudding.

What I saw and participated in there: We'd hear the radio calls for the line companies in trouble, or when they spotted some people going into a building, and we'd be assigned that fire mission and we'd destroy the building with our mortars.

I set the timers, I set the rounds, the charges for the mortars. I was part of the team that sent those rounds down range. This isn't army to army. People live in towns. I never really saw the effects of my mortar rounds in the towns, and that leaves my imagination open to countless deaths. I don't know how many civilians—innocents—I've killed, or helped to kill.

Another big piece of weaponry they used on this little town of Samawa was called a Spectre Gunship AC-130, with two belt-fed Howitzer cannons and some Super Gatling guns. They would sweep around, just pounding the city. It is definitely a sight to be seen. Even though the rounds are coming from up in the sky, it's almost like the ground is shaking. Over neighborhoods, Kiowa attack helicopters with their Hellfire missiles, F-18s dropped bombs that would shake you to the bone. All the while, I was laying down mortar fire on this town full of people.

And the radio—a good thing never came over the radio. One time they said to fire on all taxicabs because the enemy was using them for transportation. In Iraq, any car can be a taxi cab; you just paint it white and orange. One of the snipers replied back, "Excuse me? Did I hear that right? Fire on all taxi cabs?" The lieutenant colonel responded, "You heard me, trooper, fire on all taxi cabs." After that, the town lit up, with all the units firing on cars. This was my first experience with war, and that kind of set the tone for the rest of the deployment.

We were outside of a water treatment plant in Baghdad, and it seemed like a pretty nice area. As we were leaving, two men with RPGs ran out in front of us, blocking the road. There was a lot of yelling and screaming and they huddled with women and children, and we screamed back at them, "Drop your weapon, drop your weapon." I had my sight on a dude with an RPG on his back. I had my sight on his chest. This is what I'm trained to do. But when I looked at his face, he wasn't a bogeyman. He wasn't the enemy. He was scared and confused, probably the same expression I had on my face during the same time. He was probably fed the same BS I was fed. I'd seen his face, and it took me back and I didn't pull the trigger. He got away.

With the raids: We never went on a raid where we got the right house, much less the right person, not once. There's a long history in Iraq, where if you've got beef with your neighbor, you'd say, "Hey, police. They said something bad about Saddam. Why don't you go get them," and they'd take them and they'd torture them. Now here we were, asking who the troublemakers were. We'd hear "These people are the troublemakers, over here."

In this nice little village, another soldier and I toss this guy's hut. The only thing I found was a little .22-cal pistol, not AK-47s, not RPGs, not pictures of Saddam, not large caches of money. We ended up arresting the two young men regardless.

I looked at my sergeant and said, "Sergeant, these aren't the men we're looking for." He told me, "Don't worry, I'm sure they would have done something anyways." This mother all the while is crying in my face, trying to kiss my feet. I can't speak Arabic, but I can speak human. She was saying, "Please, why are you taking my sons? They have done nothing wrong." That made me feel very powerless. 82nd Airborne Infantry with Apache helicopters, Bradley fighting vehicles, armor, and my M-4. But I was powerless. I was powerless to help her. The lack of humanity in war. The place you put yourself is, when you're looking back at it, it's almost alien.

We were driving around Baghdad one day and found a dead body on the side of the road. We pulled over to secure it and waited for MPs to come and take care of this dead man who was clearly murdered. My friends jumped off and started taking pictures with him with big old smiles on their faces. They said, "Hey Viges, you want a picture with this guy?"

"No," I said. But no, not in the context of that's really messed up and just wrong on an ethical basis. I said no because it wasn't my kill. You shouldn't take trophies for things you didn't kill. That was my mindset back then. I wasn't even upset that this man was dead. They shouldn't have been taking credit for something they didn't do. But that's war. That's war.

Former U.S. Army Specialist and conscientious objector Hart Viges told the crowd at Winter Soldier he was no longer a soldier, but a "soulja."
PHOTO: MIKE HASTIE

Instead of a soldier, I'm a "soulja" now, you know. I've switched it around. I'd like to just give this little poem now:

A soulja has put down their rifles and has picked up their souls.
    Instead of bullets, a soulja has their words.
Instead of dogma, a soulja listens to their heart.
Instead of secret codes, a soulja reflects their feelings and their thoughts.
Instead of stealing land, a soulja expands their intellect.
Instead of taking aim, a soulja takes reason.
Instead of building fortifications that divide,
    a soulja grows with unity for all humankind.

And that's what I feel we're doing now.

RACISM AND THE DEHUMANIZATION OF THE ENEMY

National Guardsman Christopher Arendt: "I would like to share with you how one goes about becoming a concentration camp guard without ever having really made many decisions."

PHOTO: MIKE HASTIE

INTRODUCTION

Whenever incidents that spotlight the gross inhumanity of the U.S. occupation of Iraq leak into the media, they're quickly dismissed as isolated incidents, condemned by generals and politicians alike. "The actions of these few people do not reflect the hearts of the American people," President Bush intoned after the Abu Ghraib prison scandal broke in 2004. "What took place in that prison does not represent the America that I know." The president also promised a swift investigation, promising those responsible would be "brought to justice."[1]

Two years later, the same kinds of comments came from Washington after *Time* magazine reported the massacre of twenty-four Iraqi civilians in Haditha. U.S. military spokesman Major General William Caldwell told reporters that while "temptation exists to lump all these incidents together...each case needs to be examined individually."[2]

Administration and Pentagon officials refuse to investigate why similar acts of brutality occur again and again, because they know that kind of thoughtful inquiry would lead to a damning indictment of the occupation itself. That's why, throughout the U.S. occupations of Iraq and Afghanistan, administration and Pentagon officials have assiduously avoided asking questions implicitly raised by veterans at Winter Soldier: Why do these seemingly senseless killings occur? What makes them possible? What brings otherwise normal young men and women to the point of committing terrible atrocities? As you'll see in the chapter that follows, the answer begins with the dehumanizing nature of military training itself.

Twenty-three-year-old Robert Zabala joined the Marine Corps thinking it would be a "place where he could find security" after the death of his grandmother. But when he began boot camp in June 2003, Zabala said he was appalled by the Marine Corps' attempts to desensitize the recruits to violence.

"The response that all the recruits are supposed to say is 'kill,'" he told San Francisco's KGO-TV. "So in unison you have maybe 400 recruits chanting 'kill, kill, kill,' and after a while that word becomes almost nothing to you. What does it mean? You say it so often you really don't think of the consequences of what it means to say 'kill' over and over again as you're performing this deadly technique, a knife to the throat."[3]

When Zabala realized he couldn't kill another human being, he submitted an application for conscientious objector status to the Marine Corps Reserve. But Zabala's platoon commander denied his request: "What did you think you were joining, the Peace Corps?" court documents quote Major R.D. Doherty as saying. "I don't know how anyone who joins the Marine Corps cannot know that it involves killing."

Zabala sued and on March 29, 2007, a federal judge in Northern California overruled the military justice system, ordering the Marine Corps to discharge Zabala as a conscientious objector within fifteen days. In his ruling, U.S. District Court Judge James Ware noted Zabala's experiences with his first commander, Captain Sanchez. During basic training, Sanchez repeatedly gave speeches about "blowing shit up" or "kicking some fucking ass." In 2003, when a fellow recruit committed suicide on the shooting range, Sanchez commented in front of the recruits, "fuck him, fuck his parents for raising him, and fuck the girl who dumped him."

Another boot camp instructor showed recruits a "motivational clip" displaying Iraqi corpses, explosions, gun fights, and rockets set to a heavy-metal song that included the lyrics, "Let the bodies hit the floor," the petition said. Zabala said he cried while other recruits nodded their heads in time to the beat.[4]

This pattern of abusive, reflexive, purposely dehumanizing training is not unique to the Iraq war, the Marine Corps, or Robert Zabala. It's the way the U.S. military has trained its troops for fifty years, the results of research published by the noted military historian, U.S. Army Brigadier

General S.L.A. Marshall, who surveyed veterans after World War II.

General Marshall asked these average soldiers what they did in battle. Unexpectedly, he discovered that for every hundred men along the line of fire in battle, only fifteen to twenty actually discharged their weapons. "The average healthy individual," Marshall wrote, "has such an inner and unusually unrealized resistance toward killing a fellow man that he will not of his own volition take life if it is possible to turn away from that responsibility. ... At the vital point [the soldier] becomes a conscientious objector."[5]

Marshall's findings shocked the military and caused the Armed Forces to change their training regimen dramatically. By the Vietnam War, Pentagon studies showed 90 percent of servicemembers in combat fired their weapons.

Forcing new recruits to chant "kill, kill, kill" became common practice. The idea was to have the idea of death drilled so deeply in the mind of the servicemember that when he or she was asked to take another human life, it didn't bother them. The military also began conditioning soldiers to develop a reflexive "quick shoot" ability. In training, recruits were taught to fire their weapons without thinking about who might be killed.

"Instead of lying prone on a grassy field calmly shooting at a bulls-eye target," Army Lieutenant Colonel David Grossman wrote in his book *On Killing*, "the modern soldier spends many hours standing in a foxhole, with full combat equipment draped about his body looking over an area of lightly wooded rolling terrain. At periodic intervals one or two olive-drab, man-shaped targets at varying vantages will pop up in front of him for a brief time and the soldier will instantly aim and shoot at the targets."[6]

The idea is to dehumanize the enemy. "Under such conditions," wrote the noted Stanford University psychologist Philip Zimbardo, "it becomes possible for normal, morally upright and even idealistic people to perform acts of destructive cruelty."[7]

The result of this training can be seen every day in Iraq and Afghanistan. In a May 2007 Pentagon survey of U.S. troops in combat in Iraq, less than half of soldiers and marines said they felt they should treat noncombatants with respect. Only about half said they would report a member of their unit for killing or wounding an innocent civilian. More than 40 percent supported the idea of torture.

Overt, institutionalized racism from the command also plays an important role in distancing soldiers and marines from the people they kill. This system did not begin with the occupation of Iraq or inside the U.S. military. It is as old as war itself. In the 1930s, Nazi propaganda films depicted Jews as rodents. During the Rwandan genocide, ethnic Tutsis referred to the Hutus they slaughtered as "insects" or cockroaches. During the 1960s and '70s, American soldiers dehumanized the Vietnamese people by calling them "gooks." Today, members of the U.S. Armed Forces regularly refer to Iraqi and Afghan civilians as "hajis" and "towel-heads."

This dehumanizing group pressure is so strong that even Arabs and Muslims inside the Armed Forces adopt racial epithets to describe the "enemy." During the Racism and Dehumanization panels at Winter Soldier, David Hassan sat in the back of the room nodding in agreement. The former marine, whose father is Egyptian, had grown out his beard and wore a black-and-white checkered keffiyeh around his head. He served in Anbar province doing electronic surveillance and translated interrogations in 2005.

"I used the word [haji]," Hassan told me. "The military's not just a job, it's a culture. It pervades every aspect of your life and when you're surrounded by it 24 hours a day the culture seeps into you, and I guess—in retrospect—I had to adopt the dehumanizing of the Iraqi people to be okay with what I was a part of."

But like the other veterans at Winter Soldier, Hassan said he couldn't be a part of that dehumanization anymore. "I feel an obligation to speak out against this war," he said. "I feel like I was sold, for the majority of my life, a fallacious view of what war is and what war does to people and having seen that that's a lie—I have an obligation to speak out against it."

MICHAEL TOTTEN

Specialist, United States Army, Military Police, 716th Military Police Battalion, 101st Airborne Brigade

Deployment: April 2003–April 2004, Karbala

Hometown: Rochester, New York

Age at Winter Soldier: 26 years old

For the first six months of my deployment, I served as a driver for a security vehicle for my command sergeant major and my lieutenant colonel, and for the last six months I was put back in the line platoon for the 194th MP Company.

Former Specialist Michael Totten walks through the destroyed ruins of ancient Babylon.

PHOTO:
MICHAEL TOTTEN

This is me in Babylon, early on in the deployment. These are some ancient ruins, thousands of years old and this slide highlights the lack of respect that we had for the ancient culture and for the culture in Iraq, and it displays our insensitivity to the people of Iraq.

When I first arrived in Iraq, I was stationed in one of Saddam's palaces in Baghdad. I had a picture taken of me pointing to my American flag, thinking to myself, "Good job," and being very proud of my country. This highlights the arrogance that I had in this point in my life. It displays the heightened sense of importance that I felt and that many in my unit felt. This arrogance permits us to do harm to the Iraqi people and to treat them as second-class citizens.

I have a few talking points. I'm going to highlight that sense of importance and my unit's general attitude toward the Iraqi people. Then I'm going to go into some specifics.

I worked with my command sergeant major often and he would provide mission briefs and after action reviews for every mission that we were on. During many of these mission briefs, we used language such as "haji"—which is an Arabic term of endearment that the military has turned on its head. My command sergeant major, in one specific mission brief, said to the nine-person team, "Haji is an obstacle, do not let them get in our way," meaning that if they drove in front of us, drive through them.

At one point in the deployment, when I was on a convoy just north of Baghdad, I pulled over to have an MRE and refuel our trucks. It was about a six-vehicle convoy. Oftentimes kids in the surrounding community would run up to us and say, "Thank you, thank you," and welcome us with warm arms. We didn't want that kind of attention from the kids, for fear of their safety, because we knew we were targeted in that country.

In this incident, a kid was trying to cross a four-lane divided highway and was struck by a vehicle going about 65[mph]. I hopped in my truck and ran to stop traffic. A number of us, including my sergeant major, ran over there. About thirty seconds after he looked at the kid, the sergeant major said, "He's gone, move out." I wondered to myself what would have happened if this had been an American kid who was just struck?

Pre-deployment. The cultural competency training that we received can be best summed up in a sentence. "Don't touch the people of Iraq's left hand. They wipe their ass with it." That's what we got.

This next incident I'm about to describe was the day after we were engaged in an ambush where I was an arm's length away from a man who was shot in the neck, fell to the street, and died. His name was Corporal Sean Grilley. I had to lift him into my truck with my gunner, pulled down from the turret. We brought him into our truck and tried to MedEvac him. As a grenade blew up my left front tire and flattened it, I took about fifteen minutes to get back to the hospital, and at that point he bled to death. It was October 16, 2003. My lieutenant colonel, Kim Orlando, was also killed that night.

The incident I'm about to describe was the night after that event.

Our mission was, in part, to run a jail in Karbala. It wasn't for enemy prisoners of war but just for the general population prisoners. Prisoners would be brought in by the Iraqi police and we were to show "how we do things in America." On the night of October 17 in 2003, six people were brought in by the Iraqi police. The Iraqi police said these six participated in the actions the night prior, therefore they were army prisoners of war due to the coalition standards.

When these people were brought in, they already appeared to be beaten badly. They were lined up on the concrete wall and we told them to inter-lace their fingers. This is a form of control because you can grab your middle finger and your index finger and squeeze them together, and it's quite painful: "Interlace your fingers, place your foreheads on the concrete wall, cross your ankles, put your hands on top of your head so we can search and process you." They were tagged. They were searched. They were also beaten, not just by Americans, but by Bulgarian soldiers, Polish soldiers, Iraqi police, and by me.

I grabbed a man by the jaw and I looked him in the eye and I slammed his head against the wall. I looked him in the eye again and said, "You must have been the one that killed Grilley." Then he fell. I kicked him. An Iraqi policeman probably the size of the biggest security man here with hands to match—the size of a Kodiak—hit a guy in the side of the head at least six times. I looked at him and I laughed. I'm like, "These guys are getting what they deserve." This all took place in the presence of my lieutenant, within earshot of many NCOs. I never found out what happened to any of these people, these six prisoners. I don't know where they went, I don't know anything about that.

I'm up here today to speak on behalf of all the people who haven't re-turned home, who can't speak. This isn't just some isolated incident. It's happened in the presence of NCOs, commissioned officers, and coalition forces, not only as participants but also as witnesses.

My being up here displays my anger on multiple levels: at the Americans' behavior overseas, at our president's continuous rhetoric about Iraq being a success, at this country's citizens' apathy toward this occupation.

This is why I'm here today as well. These events happened in our name, and each and every single one of you are responsible for them.

I am very sorry for my actions. I can't take back what I did. I ask the forgiveness of the people of Iraq and of my country. I will not enable this any further.

General Petraeus, you may not remember me, but you once led me. You're no longer a leader of men. You've exploited your troops for your own gain, and have become just another cheerleader for this occupation policy that is destroying America.

General Petraeus, you pinned a Bronze Star on me in Babylon in 2003 following the October 16 incident. I will no longer be a puppet for your personal gain and for your political career. Thank you.

At the conclusion of his testimony, former Specialist Michael Totten ripped up the citation he received for his Bronze Star for Valor.

PHOTO: MIKE HASTIE

[At the conclusion of his testimony Specialist Michael Totten ripped up the citation he received for his Bronze Star for Valor. The citation, which was signed by General David Petraeus, reads: "Totten's team engaged enemy forces without regard for their personal safety, thereby removing the threat to women and children throughout the community. Private First Class Totten repeatedly exposed himself to enemy fire as his unit restored order and control back to the region, while saving countless lives. His courage, bravery, and selfless service under hostile conditions reflects great credit on him, the 101st Airborne Division, and the United States Army."]

MICHAEL LEDUC

Corporal, Marine Corps, Assaultman, Weapons
    Platoon, Charlie Company, 1st Battalion,
    8th Marines

Deployment: June–December 2004,
    Anbar, Haditha, Fallujah

Hometown: Boston, Massachusetts

Age at Winter Soldier: 22 years old

Toward the end of October 2004, my company was called into the outskirts of Camp Fallujah to an area called the Iraqi Training Center (ITC). We were being marshaled there along with several other battalions from both the army and the Marine Corps for what was going to be the second invasion of Fallujah, known as Operation Phantom Fury.

We trained there until the invasion, and one day the battalion JAG officer—the battalion's final authority on the Uniform Code of Military Justice (UCMJ)—pulled us all together, made sure the embedded reporters weren't there, and gave us our Rules of Engagement brief for Fallujah. The bottom line was that now the decision as to what "hostile action" and "hostile intent" was would be left to even the most junior of noncommissioned officers. They also pushed a tactic called reconnaissance by fire, which meant if for any reason we felt unsafe or unsure going in to clear a house or a building, we were granted the ability to do anything we wanted to that house before we entered it.

This was a really big switch from what we'd been used to. We had been using "the escalation of force," where we responded to a situation with deadly force only under very specific conditions. But now, we were operating under the assumption that everyone was hostile.

The battalion JAG officer wrapped up by sort of going, "Okay, marines, you see an individual with a weapon, what do you do?"

We mutter in silence for a minute, waiting for somebody else to answer, and one guy said, "Shoot him?"

"No. Shooting at a target, putting rounds down range and suppressing a target, is one thing. Sighting and killing a target is another. So again, you see an individual with a weapon, what do you do?"

"Kill him."

"You see an individual with a pair of binoculars, what do you do?"

"Kill him."

"You see an individual with a cell phone out, what do you do?"

"Kill him."

"You see an individual who although may not be actually carrying anything or displaying any specific hostile action or intent running from, say, one building to another, running across the street or even running away from you, assume that he is maneuvering against you and kill him. You see an individual with a white flag and he does anything but approach you slowly and obey commands, assume it's a trick and kill him."

Fallujah: we went by those ROEs. Fighting was fairly intense for the first few days especially. Leveling houses before we even went in became pretty commonplace, using bulldozers and tanks to do the job for us, and walking through the rubble.

After the first few days, things began to calm down. We'd be holed up in houses for a few hours or maybe a day or two and we'd get bored. We'd get angry and be like, "Let's break stuff." We ran out of people to shoot, so we turned to dogs and cats, chickens, whatever's moving. Some guys, they'd name the bodies left out in the street. Rotten Randy. Tony the Torso. Some people would adjust the sights on their rifles, using the heads of people laid out in the street. Just fire a shot, if it hit too far to the left, adjust the sight and shoot again.

I remember one instance where we were on the roof of a mosque that had just been taken maybe a day before. It was daylight, and not too far away there was a house where an entire family seemed to have been holed up in a basement for a while. There were a few men, a few women, and a bunch of kids. What their coming out and waving signified to me was they were trying to let us know that they were there, and they were unarmed. One of the marines on scene reacted by shooting at them. I don't know if he was specifically aiming at them. None of them got hit but they just ran back in. We never saw them again.

I remember hanging out in houses and then we'd start going through stuff. We'd look through family photo albums and pictures of the house and the neighborhood. We'd compare it to what it looked like now and have a good laugh.

One night, we were going out to occupy a house as an observation point. The city sewer system had been damaged by bombs and the streets had been flooded with sewer water. As the fighting went on, the water filled up with dead bodies, so it was pretty horrible. The day before, several people had been shot and they detained the rest of the people that they found, including the wife of one of the men who was killed. Either her uncle or father was blind. On our way to this observation point, we were supposed to escort them back to the house. They were lagging behind. They were holding us up. Halfway there, we just left them there, standing in the middle of the flooded streets, and went on to our objective.

I joined the military with the intention of contributing something positive, to do something good to improve the whole human situation. I felt that Iraq was a good place to do that. I was very young and naive, and I was wrong. I won't say that I'm overly wrought by anything that happened. There were some times when I got to do what I wanted to do and I felt good about myself a few times. For the most part, I was just doing what I had to do and that was all of us, whether it was breaking the rules or following them, whether it was doing what I thought was right or doing what I knew was wrong.

SCOTT EWING

Specialist, United States Army, Cavalry Scout, Third Cavalry Division

Deployment: March 2005–March 2006, Tal Afar

Hometown: Pawtucket, Rhode Island

Age at Winter Soldier: 38 years old

We spent most of our time in Tal Afar, a city of about two hundred thousand people just west of Mosul in northern Iraq. In March 2006, President Bush described our deployment as a model of counterinsurgency operations, calling Tal Afar "a free city that gives reason for hope for a free Iraq." The media pounced on this with criticism of his optimistic assertion. For one thing, we had driven out thousands of Sunnis and created a more homogenous population of predominantly Shia tribes.

Additionally, by the end of our deployment, we had about a thousand troops per square kilometer in the city. Between then and now, Tal Afar has seen some of the most violent and deadly attacks of this occupation.

When we first arrived at Camp Sykes, there were frequent attacks on U.S. forces. I was in a scout platoon. Initially we did fairly simple operations: "over watch" missions to try to detect people placing IEDs on main supply routes and patrols in neighborhoods that were viewed as relatively safe. My job was to get out of the Bradley, stand next to it, and provide security.

One of the first things we noticed when we entered Tal Afar is that kids approached our vehicles fairly fearlessly. I asked my interpreter why and he told me they wanted soccer balls. Apparently, the unit before us had frequently taken soccer balls out and given them to the kids. Soon, we began to bring candy out in bags and the guys up in the turret of the Bradleys would throw it out the sides of the vehicle. The kids all rushed to the sides of the vehicle and hung out and fought for the candy. It was billed as a gesture of goodwill. There was also another motive: If the kids were around our vehicles, the bad guys wouldn't attack. We used the kids as human shields.

Not long after we got to Tal Afar, we were told that two rival tribes had fought over control of the hospital in the city. The tribe that currently controlled the hospital, we were told, wanted us to provide security for it. So we started doing rotations at the hospital. There were already Iraqi army troops on the roof, inside the hospital, and at the gates. At first, we took over a room on the ground floor with hospital beds in it and that's where we stayed.

As soon as we arrived, the hospital was attacked and the Iraqi army troops on the roof fired wildly into the neighborhoods. So within the few hours of us arriving, the hospital saw patients. A man came in shot through the chest; a boy came in shot through the leg. And the cycle repeated. Every time we would go out, people would mortar the hospital, shoot RPGs and small-arms fire, and normally the Iraqi army would fire back.

Eventually somebody suggested that staying in the hospital as a fighting force might be a violation of the Geneva Conventions. It was a sergeant who suggested that in the presence of an officer. And a few days later we moved to a government building about fifty feet away from the hospital. The hospital was still mortared because mortars are not very precise. Even when they were shooting at the government building fifty feet away, we were still drawing fire into the hospital.

Eventually, the first soldier in my platoon was killed by an RPG. After that, my unit left the hospital and moved to a different area of the city. Another unit in the regiment took over operations there and the Iraqi army troops remained stationed inside the hospital, on the roof, and at the front gate, under the guidance of American advisors.

In September 2005 we began a two-week-long mission *Time* magazine dubbed "The Battle of Tal Afar." The army called this Operation Restoring Rights. The idea was to search the entire city, house by house, block by block, and clear it of weapons. Up until that point, we had permitted every adult male Iraq to keep one AK-47 for self-defense. With about two hundred thousand residents and several million dark windows from which to shoot, this wasn't working well. So we swept through the city with around eight thousand Iraqi and American troops and began to search every house. We sometimes knocked down their front gates with our Bradleys, and occasionally blew them off the hinges with explosives. But usually we went from rooftop to rooftop and entered their homes from above. We separated the men from the women and the children, questioned people, checked their

IDs, collected their weapons, and did fairly light searches of the houses.

At the same time, we cordoned off the southeast corner of the city, which was known as the Sari neighborhood. We had been repeatedly told that this neighborhood was an insurgent stronghold, so we gave the residents an order to evacuate their homes and provided camps outside the city for them to stay in. After that, we bombed their neighborhood for several days and nights using AC-130 Spectre Gunships, Apache helicopters, and tank rounds. The idea was that the insurgents would stay behind and fight while the civilians left. On September 10, the Kurdish militias entered Sari with U.S. Special Forces to clear the neighborhood of any remaining insurgents. As they began moving through, our troops entered to gather evidence of the insurgency and, in particular, of foreign fighters.

We were told to search Sari aggressively, to teach the residents a lesson: Don't harbor terrorists. We knocked down doors, dumped drawers out, pushed furniture over, broke windows, and generally trashed the homes. In the end, my platoon found absolutely no evidence of foreign fighters; no weapons caches except common household items. This is a representative photograph of "evidence" of the insurgency. I was asked to take this photograph by the commissioned officer on the scene.

A photograph of "evidence" of the insurgency collected during a raid in Tal Afar.

PHOTO: SCOTT EWING

I remember someone said, "The saws might be used by terrorists to dismember bodies." And the officer standing nearby asked suggestively, "Seriously, why would anyone have this many saws?" As though having wood saws was suspicious. In the end, we photographed kitchen knives, wood saws, some ragged old pistol belts, and empty bottles of antibiotics. After we had searched the entire Sari neighborhood ahead of schedule and found no resistance, someone in the chain of command came up with another suggestion. "Maybe the insurgents somehow escaped north to another neighborhood just past our checkpoints."

So, we struck out on September 12 and sent the Kurdish militia in to round up every military-aged male from every house in another section of the city. We sat about five hundred men down in a large, barbed wire enclosure and stood guard as the families all gathered on the other side of the street. At that point, one of our interpreters sent a single anonymous, masked man in desert camouflage up and down the lines of men. He either gave a thumbs up or a thumbs down before each man he passed. Thumbs up meant the guy was a terrorist, thumbs down meant he wasn't. In this way, we detained about fifty men from the group, zip-tied them, and in some cases wrote their alleged crime—"Cuts heads," for instance—on their arm with a permanent marker. Another commissioned officer, Captain Noah Hanners, wrote "Cuts heads" on a detainee's forearm and is quoted in the September 13, 2005, edition of the *Washington Post* as saying, "You get treated special today, buddy."

One of the other statements made in the press around this time was by our squadron commander, Lieutenant Colonel Christopher Hickey. He was quoted in the *Washington Post* as saying, "We lose these people if we go in there and tear people's homes apart," which makes sense to me. It's consistent with counterinsurgency doctrine, which places an emphasis on winning the support of the local population. But after Operation Restoring Rights ended, we continued our aggressive search tactics.

I decided to e-mail Lieutenant Colonel Hickey recently and I asked him about this. He replied, "The way you described being aggressive in our search, I would characterize as being disrespectful and counterproductive to what we were trying to do. I do not support tactics that ransacked homes."

So where did things go wrong? There is no question that we ransacked homes and did so under orders. Equally, it's clear to me that this kind of behavior was not consistent with counterinsurgency doctrine, in which Colonel H.R. McMaster, the commander of our regiment, was clearly well versed.

I have to conclude that even in the best of situations in Iraq, civilians still die, questionable decisions are still made, the insurgency still rages, and in the end the only war our country has waged well is a propaganda war on its own people.

JEFFREY SMITH

Specialist, United States Army, Florida Army
   National Guard, Infantry, Bravo Company,
   2nd of the 124th Infantry

Deployment: February 2003–January 2004,
   Kuwait, Qatar, Balad

Hometown: Orlando, Florida

Age at Winter Soldier: 36 years old

I was a military brat. My father served two tours in Vietnam and is currently rated 100 percent disabled by the Veterans Administration due to PTSD and Agent Orange exposure.

When I deployed to Balad, my unit was tasked with gate and perimeter security at Camp Anaconda, the largest of the enduring bases in Iraq. We were tasked with clearing Iraqi nationals who worked on post, doing such jobs as filling sand bags, clearing rubble and trash, etc.

These Iraqi nationals were paid a dollar a day and were given an MRE for lunch. They worked under extreme conditions of heat and dust, oftentimes 130-degree temperature, and were always escorted by armed guards. Every morning, the Iraqis that wanted to come on post to work were herded into a barbed wire enclosure. Almost every day, they would start pushing each other into the barbed wire. In order to get them to stop doing that, we used physical force. This included shoving, stroking Iraqis with the butts of our weapons, and threatening them with bayonets. There were several occasions when we locked and loaded our weapons and told them if they didn't stop pushing each other that we were going to open fire.

One of our other responsibilities at the front gate was to search the several hundred dump trucks and semitrailers that were coming on post every day. The dump trucks were also driven by Iraqis. We usually had one or two interpreters on duty with us, but inevitably there would be miscommunication.

One day, an Iraqi dump truck driver didn't understand that he was supposed to stop and continued forward in his truck. My team leader interpreted this as a hostile action, ran over, yanked him out of the truck, and the rest of my team responded. We beat the crap out of this guy, pushed him down in the dirt, detained him, roughed him up, and told him that he was not allowed to come back on the post for at least a month. I don't know what he did for the next month.

We also raided houses. One of the first houses we raided was supposedly the home of a former Ba'ath official. It was the middle of the day when we arrived in the neighborhood. The raid started when the armored cavalry unit that was with us rolled over the front wall of the house. I was second in the stack formation of troops that went through the gate. There was an older female who was in the courtyard and she was screaming something unintelligible in Arabic. One of the soldiers behind me apparently thought that she was a threat. He butt stroked her in the face, knocked her to the ground, and someone after him zip-tied her and took her out into the front yard.

We proceeded to ransack this house. I was in the master bedroom. There were dressers and wardrobes; the wardrobes were locked. We pulled the doors off. We turned everything in the room upside down. We went through everything. Personnel in my unit that were in the kitchen turned the refrigerator upside down and broke the stove: pulled it out of the wall, broke the line to it. After, we searched through the house and we had everyone including the children zip-tied on the front lawn. Then someone in my chain of command realized that we had the wrong home. We were on the wrong street. The home we were supposed to have raided was actually behind this house on another street.

So we went and raided that house. Going through the gate of that home, I almost fired on a person that was mentally disabled. He was standing in a window directly in front of us and he didn't understand what was going on. I almost fired and then realized that there was something wrong with him and he just didn't realize what was happening.

We searched through that home, detained the person that we were supposed to detain, and started coming across all this paperwork in his office and his bedroom. It looked to me like he was an algebra instructor, maybe at the local high school, maybe at a local university, because there were reams of paper that were just math problems. This guy was supposed to be a former Ba'ath official.

We took him, put a sandbag over his head, loaded him on a truck, and started back toward Camp Anaconda. He was on my vehicle with my squad and on the way back to Camp Anaconda—it was about a forty-five-minute drive—my squad leader thought that it would be funny to pose for a picture next to this guy. He asked me to take a photo of him and this detainee, but I refused to do so. Upon arrival back at our quarters, I was disciplined, including physical punishment, because I had disobeyed him in front of the rest of the squad.

The turning point for me in Iraq was an incident that occurred when I was off duty at night. There was a "hard core" platoon in my company. Every unit has one platoon that is more extreme than the rest. This platoon happened to have a squad that was attacked while they were hiding out in the farms in the surrounding area, trying to detain people who were out past curfew.

They were out there one night and a farmer was on his property. It was 3 a.m., but because electricity is intermittent, there was work that he couldn't do during the day. He was out there trying to work on a pump. They told him to stop. He panicked and ran. They opened fire and killed this individual. The next day, civil affairs came and spoke with our company and said, "We are not going to pay any benefit to this family." They also informed us that his brother was our close ally. Until this time he had been working with us and was a respected leader of the local community. They also said the individual we killed had fourteen children. The civil affairs officer suggested that we take up a collection and donate a dollar or two apiece to the family and that he thought that that would go a long way in helping to ease the family's suffering. There's roughly 125 members of a rifle company, so you're talking about anywhere between $125 and $150. I don't think anyone donated any money.

Oftentimes we would be called out as a quick-reaction force to respond to incidents in the town of Balad. On these patrols through the town, my squad leader would entertain himself by shooting the local animals, including dogs that were tied up in people's front yards. There was one occasion where he started shooting dogs. The lieutenant came over the radio, said, "What's going on? Why are you firing? What's happening?" My squad leader indicated that he was just shooting dogs and my lieutenant replied back, "Well, that's okay but from now on let me know that you're gonna do that before you do it."

Finally—this is probably the hardest incident for me to talk about: One morning, a few months prior to me leaving, I was on the last security post behind the front gate. I was manning a machine gun that was there to ensure that if anyone managed to get past the front gate that they wouldn't actually get inside the post. It was very early in the morning and I was haggard and not in a very good mood. I saw a Humvee come through the gate towing a blue mini pickup truck. Those were very common in Iraq. From a distance I couldn't really tell what was going on. As they approached, it appeared that the pickup truck was riddled with bullets and shrapnel; I think one of the tires was flat.

Apparently there had been an attack on a convoy earlier that morning using this pickup truck. As the Humvee pulled past, I realized that the pickup truck was full of dead people killed in this attack. They had obviously been engaged with large-caliber weapons, probably Mark 19s, .50 caliber. There were several decapitated corpses with large holes through their bodies.

I'll never forget this. There was a very young PFC, I believe, standing in the back of the pickup truck. As they rolled by, he lifted one of the decapitated heads up in front of me and he said, in much rougher language, "We really screwed these guys up, didn't we?" There was another enlisted member in the back of the truck with him, and they were celebrating on top of these bodies piled up in the back. These "insurgents" didn't appear to me to look like the hardened terrorists that everyone says they are. These were mostly teenage boys and young men who looked like they were from the local community.

I want to take this time to apologize to the Iraqi people for the things that I helped to do and the actions that people in my unit and myself did while I was there.

BRYAN CASLER

Corporal, United States Marine Corps, Rifleman, 2nd Battalion, 6th Marines, Fox Company

Deployments: 2003, from Kuwait to Babylon; 2004–2005, Kabul, Afghanistan; 2005–2006, Fallujah

Hometown: Syracuse, New York

Age at Winter Soldier: 24 years old

I want to talk about some of the smaller things that occurred very frequently throughout my three combat tours. These are things that I left out of the letters home and I rarely mention because they're not things I'm proud of. Whether I participated or I witnessed it, I never stopped it.

When I first arrived at the fleet after completing infantry training, I checked into my unit, and we had our first company formation. I didn't think about it until I had made friends with a few people, but our first platoon was a segregated platoon. Nearly 90 percent of all minorities in the company had been moved to 1st Platoon, where white leaders were put in charge as squad leaders and platoon sergeant. After I had been in the Marine Corps a couple years, it became apparent that minorities in our unit were not being promoted at the same rate as whites. The ones that did get promoted were exceptional. They would have been promoted no matter where they were because they went through meritorious boards. They were some of the brightest and best marines I've ever worked with.

Some common things you'll face in your daily non-combat environment. If you're in an office and it's the morning, and you're walking by one of your staff sergeants and you say, "Good morning, staff sergeant." I guess the common response in the civilian world would be, "Good morning to you, too." But in the Marine Corps, you get, "Er, kill babies." That's motivating. That's not meant to be funny. That's meant to motivate you and start off your day with, "Er, kill babies." And this isn't something that just happens once. The Marine Corps is filled with one-upmanship to say the most dehumanizing, racist, most offensive thing, and to enjoy it while you're doing it.

I was deployed to Kuwait in support of the invasion of Iraq. Once the invasion kicked off, we crossed the border into Iraq. We had a mostly positive reception by the Iraqi people. But on these convoys, I saw marines defecate into MRE bags or urinate in bottles and throw them at children on the side of the road. When we stopped, marines would take out their MRE bag, remove the moisture-activated chemical heater that we use to heat MREs. They would remove the chemical heater from the package that said, "Do not eat," with a symbol of a person and an X sign through them, and they would give that to Iraqi children to see the response on their faces.

We didn't have a clearly defined mission except to keep pushing forward. When you don't have a clearly defined mission, the mission becomes to come home alive, to survive. Marines love nothing more than to one-up each other by using their training, and when you become stagnant and the mission becomes survival, marines use their training on marines around them or on the civilian population. I saw our training for protesters or violent situations used on unsuspecting civilians countless times, because there were no rules. This was perpetrated by squad leaders and platoon sergeants. It happened all the time.

My second combat deployment was to guard the United States Embassy in Kabul, Afghanistan. In Afghanistan, we were told we were going to become leaders, that we were going to step up and start taking leadership positions. The point of the matter is that we would be unsupervised, because we were the leadership. Well, this was more viewed as a time to have some fun with our un-supervision and do what boys do.

One of the first things we did as leaders was to drive to a range in white vans. Some people who didn't even have licenses back in the States or know how to drive stick were now driving these vans through the crowded downtown streets of Kabul, Afghanistan at extremely high speeds, as fast as the vehicles would go. Driving into oncoming traffic, driving between the two lanes, pushing vehicles out of the way. On one occasion, a man was killed coming through an intersection at speeding vehicles. He was hit by the vehicle; he was not shot. Our vehicle hit this man and we kept driving. I do not know if his family received reparations or any repayment from the U.S. government.

Another time one of the drivers without a license hit a man and his donkey on a cart. That was an entire family's livelihood, and that family could have been ruined by this one small incident.

I returned to Iraq for my third deployment in 2005. We were stationed in downtown Fallujah, at the mayor's compound. We had a couple marines that were being punished and one of their punishments was to remove all the paperwork from the top floor of the mayor's compound and bring it down to our dumpsters while in full gear. This took hours, and I think it might have spanned across days. Well, after all the paperwork was gone, I finally had a chance to sit down with my interpreter and ask, "What was all that paperwork?" Well, we destroyed all the birth certificates for the city of Fallujah.

I'd also like to talk about an important story a lot of my fellow IVAW members shared: the moment you realized you were only affected by American casualties and not Iraqi casualties. One of the roles I filled was on an ambulance that rushed to pick up wounded in the city. We were told there were Iraqi wounded and they were the police or the Iraqi military in training. I was excited. Talk to anyone that works in an ambulance or as an EMT, your adrenaline gets going. We rushed out there, our vehicle slowed down, we pulled up. There was a mass of people around a bloodied area and a blown-up vehicle. As we slowly pulled forward, I saw some desert boots and then some digital desert camouflage. I'm like, "I didn't know that the Iraqi military had this." Then we pulled farther forward and I realized that it was just another marine that had been wounded. He wasn't part of our unit. He was on a convoy going through the city, but this was the first time that I was affected in such a way. I was excited about what we were doing, and then a second later I was terrified, and it was only because an American was wounded and not an Iraqi.

I'd like to sum up what all my statements have to do with: When you have neither a clearly defined mission nor positive support, the only mission a marine infantryman knows by heart is the mission of a Marine Corps rifle squad: "Locate, close in, and destroy the enemy by fire and maneuver or to repel the enemy assault by fire and close combat." That's what you're going to do. You're going to use your training and you're going to use that one mission that you know verbatim, by heart, with your eyes closed, while you're asleep. You dream about it and you train every day, through three months of boot camp and three months of infantry training and you train between deployments and during deployments to carry out that mission.

When your mission's not defined, all you have is hammers and everything you find is nails and you're going to crush it. You're going to crush every nail you find. We're crushing the Iraqi people with the training we're given and the unsupportive nature around us in the military.

CHRISTOPHER ARENDT

Specialist, United States Army National Guard, Field Artillery, Charlie 1st in the 119th Field Artillery

Deployment: Guantánamo Bay, Cuba

Hometown: Charlotte, Michigan

Age at Winter Soldier: 23 years old

I would like to share with you how one goes about becoming a concentration camp guard without ever having really made many decisions.

I was seventeen years old when I joined the Army National Guard in Michigan. I was living with friends. I decided to join the military November 20, 2001, because I had no other options. My family was poor, I was poor, and I wanted to go to school. I was promised a significant amount of money for this purpose, which I have yet to receive.

I was in the field artillery, Charlie 1st of the 119th Field Artillery, where I served, quite happily, for…no. That's a lie. I was miserable; I hated it, but I served nonetheless.

We got orders in October 2003 that we would be deploying to Guantánamo Bay, Cuba. Artillerymen would be deploying to Guantánamo Bay, Cuba to be prison guards.

During our one-month mobilization process, we were taught how to put shackles on other people. It feels ridiculous when you are practicing how to put shackles on another human being. You realize how absurd it is. You're putting them on somebody's hands and it's awkward. It hurts, it's uncomfortable, and it feels dehumanizing. This is just practice. This is just to warm up for the big game.

We left for Guantánamo Bay early in January 2004. It was hot. It was uncomfortable. We slept in awful little houses, but at least we had houses.

I served on the blocks for two months as a prison guard. My duties were to feed detainees and dispense toilet paper. I occupied myself in some way, shape, or form to drive the boredom out. The primary difficulty in keeping my humanity intact was the boredom.

One of the ways I dealt with this was by talking with the detainees. A consequence of having detainees is that they are human beings and also have stories. I talked with them about those stories, which led to my being taken off the blocks. I was sent to work in the Detention Operations Center as the escort control for the last eight months of my tour. I managed the movements of every detainee in Camp Delta. I did this on twelve- to fourteen-hour shifts, and rotated with a very small crew of other Specialists. I was nineteen at the time.

Papers, numbers, shackles, and keys. All of that had to be accounted for, but it wasn't anything more than papers, numbers, shackles, and keys. I'd call two people in, usually outranking me, and I'd have to tell them to do something that they hated doing. And they hated me for telling them to do it.

That's the nature of the machine. We're just chips in a Plinko machine. Orders come down from God knows who or where. They just keep coming down.

There are two specific things I will address about the operation at Guantánamo Bay, Cuba. One is the issue of torture. I've heard a lot of speculation as to what torture is. I would like to ask everyone to consider whether living in a cell for five years, away from your family and friends, without ever being given answers as to why you're there, whether this is torture. Having to ask nineteen-year-old boys who don't have any idea about the policies of their government why they are detained and the answers that we weren't able to give—I consider that torture.

But if that wasn't enough, we had other methods to make certain we got around to torturing these people.

I dispatched the detainee movements. I would come into the office at 4:30 in the morning and there would sometimes be a little paper in the wall with a number on it, which represented a detainee inside of an interrogation room. The temperature of the interrogation room was maybe 10 or 20 degrees, with loud music playing. Sometimes that detainee would stay there for my entire twelve- to fourteen-hour shift. He was shackled to the floor by his hands and his feet, with nothing to sit on, loud music playing, in the freezing cold. I guess that's torture; that depends on who you ask.

I hear there is an official list of things that are and are not torture. Waterboarding is torture. My recent example is not. I can't believe a human being could even write a list like that.

The other issue I would like to address is the common usage of the Quick Reaction Force, which is a rotating five-man team established each morning. If a detainee is unsatisfied with his stay and becomes rowdy, five grown men are fitted with riot gear and lined up outside of a cell while the platoon leader of that camp sprays the detainee in the face with pepper spray. I was sprayed with pepper spray once, and I feel that's one of the worst moments in my life. It put me on my knees for two to three hours afterwards, and in a great deal of pain for the next three days. I would never, ever want anyone to have this happen to them.

After spraying the detainee, these five men would rush in and take whatever opportunities they could. The Standard Operating Procedures do not state that you should beat the shit out of detainees, but I guess that some people just decided that's what they were going to do anyway.

These are all on tape, by the way. The government makes sure that each one of these operations is taped. I taped several of them, and I would be happy to show you those clips, but I doubt they will be released anytime soon.

After the detainee is taken forcibly from his cell—that's probably the first time that he's left his cell in five, six, seven days—the detainees are beaten, pulled out to the back, shaved, all of their hair, their beard, and then taken to wherever they were supposed to go.

There was one other thing I wanted to address, about the use of the term "detainee." We were told it had to be detainee. It had to be detainee. If it's a prisoner, then they are a Prisoner of War, and subject to entirely different laws. If they're detainees, they're subject to no law whatsoever, because there aren't laws for detainees. Because they are called detainees, they don't get trials and there is no code for how they're treated. It's semantics, and we need to pay attention to those; they're important. It's the difference between calling something a detention facility and a concentration camp, even if they're the same thing.

ANDREW DUFFY

Sergeant, Iowa Army National Guard, Medic

Deployment: October 2005–October 2006, Abu Ghraib

Hometown: Iowa City, Iowa

Age at Winter Soldier: 21 years old

The first incident I would like to talk about happened on March 13, 2006, involving a detainee at Abu Ghraib's in-processing center.

The sign at the intake processing wing of Abu Ghraib prison while Andrew Duffy served there reads: "Winning the hearts and minds of the Iraqi people one detainee at a time." PHOTO: ANDREW DUFFY

That was the sign outside the in-processing center. "Winning the hearts and minds of the Iraqi people, one detainee at a time." I can tell you how we won one of those minds. My fellow medic and I were making our rounds through the in-processing center when a truckload of new captures came in. They often came in truckloads because we would arrest any military-aged male in the vicinity of an incident.

As we were going through these people, evaluating them and checking them out, one young man stood out to me as being particularly irate and kind of out of it, seemingly drunk. I felt it was necessary to take his blood sugar. Normal blood sugar is between 80 and 120 mg/dl. When I took his blood sugar, it was 431 mg/dl. The detainee could speak English very well and said he had been taking insulin and that he had been captured by the Iraqi forces, held for approximately four to five days, and during that time they had not given him his insulin. Supposedly it was in his personal effects.

I called the officer in charge of the Abu Ghraib hospital and requested that we transport this detainee. I was told twice over the phone, ordered by the captain of the 344th Combat Support Hospital, that I could not transport the detainee, and that he needed to drink water. She also stated that he was a "haji, and he probably wouldn't die, but it would not matter if he died, anyway."

In the early hours of March 14 my partner and I went back to the camp to see the same individual who was now more irate, more intoxicated looking, and sweating profusely. I called my captain again, and again was denied permission to take him to the hospital. There was little I could do, and she told us to give him water and a 14-gauge IV. A normal IV is an 18- to 20-gauge. So we did that, and then we got off our shift.

On the morning of March 15, the MPs mistook this twenty-three-year-old young man's diabetic shock for insubordination. They pepper-sprayed him and put him into a segregation cell in the sun, where he spent his last few hours. He died en route to the hospital in one of our ambulances. Captain Hogan said that we had never called her and that we had never tried to transport the detainee.

The next day, my partner and I were awoken out of our beds and told that we needed to go down and be interrogated by a CID colonel about the death of the detainee we had seen the previous night. Maybe three days after that, we were interrogated again by a lieutenant colonel, at which time I filled out a five-page sworn statement. We were cleared of everything, and Captain Hogan remained the night shift officer in charge of the hospital at Abu Ghraib.

I also have a second story that emphasizes racism and how the word "haji" is often used, similar to how a racist in this country would use the "N-word."

You see, we used different ambulances for the detainees than we did for medical support on American convoys. They had older equipment. Often the fluids or the prescription drugs would be expired, sometimes by years.

I got a call saying there was an unconscious detainee in one of the camps that usually held very docile prisoners. My partner drove while I prepared the oxygen and I attempted to prepare the Automated External Defibrillator (AED). However, my platoon sergeant ordered the wrong pads for the AED, so when I arrived on the scene I was unable to shock and revive him, which we learned later would probably have saved his life. We attempted to ventilate him on the way to the hospital but we could not. The mask was so deformed due to the heat and because it was so old. I ended up performing mouth-to-mouth resuscitation on the detainee.

A lot of people called them hajis. To me, this detainee was just an old man that could've been somebody's father, grandfather, or uncle. I remember exactly how he looked, and I remember exactly how he felt, dying in my hands. I revived him for about fifteen seconds at which point my assistant called ahead to the hospital but they didn't respond.

We got to the hospital to find them very apathetic. The two medics working the emergency room were sitting on cots, sleeping. The emergency room doctor was playing Slingo, the computer game. In the emergency room I had to continue performing mouth-to-mouth resuscitation on this detainee. I later overheard many comments about how "That medic made out with a haji." I was isolated by that incident. A lot of people came up to me and said, "How the hell could you do that?" I told them, "What if that was your grandfather or your father? Wouldn't you do the same thing?"

I could see why people wouldn't want to take care of Iraqis because, at the same time, we treated wounded U.S. soldiers. I remember a time when I treated a marine with his legs blown off who died in our care. About a half an hour later, I had to give a detainee pills for a headache. But as a medic, and as a professional, I needed to treat these people the same. They are human beings, and I couldn't treat them like subhumans.

I'll just finish up with a very short story. Me and the same medic from the first incident were called to the in-processing center where they had a semiconscious man in the back of a five-ton truck. He was restrained with his hands cuffed behind his back and his feet cuffed. He was also blindfolded. The sergeant in charge asked me if I felt the detainee could walk the approximate fifteen feet to the doorway. I revived him and said, "He could probably walk with assistance to the doorway." The sergeant picked up the blindfolded man by the flexi-cuffs, threw him off the back of the Humvee, face-down, chest-down, in the gravel, and said, "You can't spell abuse without Abu."

Andrew Duffy enlisted in the Iowa National Guard two days after he turned seventeen. At age nineteen, he was deployed to Iraq, where he served as a medic in Abu Ghraib prison.

PHOTO: MIKE HASTIE

SAM LYNCH
Specialist, North Carolina Army National Guard, Medical Specialist

Deployment: February–December 2004, Eastern Diyala Province

Hometown: Middlesex, North Carolina

Age at Winter Soldier: 32 years old

I joined the Army in 1994 as an infantryman and did active duty for a little while. In 1997 I became a conscientious objector. But I opted to stay in the military and transfer into medical services. After getting out of active duty, I went to the North Carolina National Guard and I deployed with the North Carolina National Guard to Iraq from February 2004 until December 2004.

When we first got to Camp Caldwell in late February, early March, we were occupying an area that didn't have a lot of U.S. military forces. It was an Iraqi training base and we ran operations out of there as well. So there was no established detention facility, no Standard Operating Procedure (SOP), and really nothing to establish a practice of care.

Late April, early May, I became the supervisor for the detainee medical program. I was a specialist, a rather low rank. It just turned out that I knew two or three phrases in Arabic, and no one else wanted the job. I developed an SOP to provide a daily sick call for the detainees. Medical personnel would go down every day and do a face-to-face with each detainee, see how they were doing, and treat any medical conditions they may have had.

My original plan called for a medical professional, either a physician assistant or a doctor, to go down as well. On the first day this plan went into effect, the doctors refused to go. Throughout the next eight months, only three of the fifteen doctors in our clinic would go to see the detainees. So the medics did most of the detainee medical care. Most of the things were headaches and backaches, which could be treated with Tylenol or Motrin. But there were urinary tract infections, hernias, things that really did require a doctor's care. When I confronted doctors with this, at least four different doctors responded saying they wouldn't see the detainees because they were not American.

Our detainee facility was a seventy-two-hour-tops detainee facility, where they would bring in locals who were being detained and decide whether or not they had enough evidence to push them forward to a larger detainee facility such as Abu Ghraib. So we only had them for a brief period of time.

Some specific incidents: Early on, there was a individual with blood clots in his lower legs, and it was possible that a blood clot would loosen itself and become lodged and cause a stroke. So we had him on Lovenox shots twice a day. This was right when the clinic was starting, so I was still going through and getting doctors' signatures on prescriptions. I had to do it day by day. So whether or not this person would get his medication depended on the doctor on duty. Toward the end of the rotation, it got to the point where the medics—not the doctors—were prescribing medicine for the detainees because nobody else would do it.

When we did an initial assessment of all the detainees, the MPs who ran the detainee center tended to identify the detainees by what they had been arrested for. Instead of it being an individual, they became a number. 30-0024, for example, "tried to bomb U.S. soldiers" or "is targeting translators." They lost their identity in that process and it was hard to maintain an unbiased attitude toward caring for them when the first thing you hear is what they're there for. As it turned out, a high percentage of the people who were detained were just released because there was not enough evidence. I don't have an exact number, but during the time I was supervisor, we saw approximately 225 detainees, and I would say that at least 60 or 70 percent were released for lack of evidence.

This medical neglect started to influence our treatment of other Iraqis. The Iraqi workers on the post would be doing construction work and have an injury, and they would be refused treatment. There was a translator I worked with quite often who developed a hip problem. I tried to get him an X-ray, and the doctors refused to treat him. There was a lot of neglect. Having been in charge, I feel a lot of guilt because I didn't say anything. I feel that I did these people an injustice by not demanding that the doctors actually see them, and instead allowing myself and the other medics to do the doctors' job on our own.

MATTHEW CHILDERS

Corporal, United States Marine Corps, Infantry, 1st Battalion, 4th Marines, Charlie Company, 2nd Platoon

Deployments: May–August 2003, al-Hilla; May 2004–February 2005, al-Najaf

Hometown: Onia, West Virginia

Age at Winter Soldier: 23 years old

Between April and August of 2003, 1st Battalion 4th Marines was occupying a pistol factory in al-Hilla, and my platoon was tasked with detainee watch. There were three detainees in our custody for about a week. Over this week they were beaten relentlessly, humiliated, and teased with food and water. They begged the marines for food and water and the marines mocked them, throwing water in their faces. The detainees were flexi-cuffed with their wrists behind their back, and they were blindfolded.

The marines screamed at them to get up and then they'd trip them down on their face. The detainees couldn't break their fall 'cause they were tied up. The marines showed the Iraqis pornography, which was strictly taboo to their religion. I saw a marine take the hat off of an Iraqi. He shoved it down the back of his pants and wiped himself with it and then tried to feed it to the Iraqi who was blindfolded. Because he was so desperate for food, the Iraqi actually tried to eat it.

These guys were in our custody for about a week and I didn't see them eat the whole time. I wasn't around them 24/7 and I don't know how long the posts were but I didn't see them eat or sleep at all. I remember the marines taking this flexi-cuffed guy out to use the restroom. He was wearing a dishdasha and was trying to squat to spread his gown so he could use the bathroom. But the marines kept kicking him in the ankles. His ankles were bloody. They shoved him over while he was trying to use the restroom, telling him that he should stand up and urinate like a man.

During both tours in Iraq, there was an obvious and intentional dehumanization of the Iraqis. We raided countless residences. Most of the time we'd show up, at like 3 a.m. in the early hours of the morning, bust into the house, systematically clear every room, pointing semiautomatic and automatic weapons in their faces, and screaming at them in a language they didn't understand. I don't know where the intelligence was coming from, but we barely ever found anything in these houses.

While searching the people taken from their homes, a lot of times the marines would hit them in the genitals or poke them with the muzzle of their rifle.

At the pistol factory during my first deployment in al-Hilla, I was on the front-entry checkpoint to the forward operating base with a fellow marine. We were having a conversation. We weren't really paying attention, and suddenly there was a man fifteen feet away carrying a baby. All the baby's skin was burned off. The man was very upset. He wanted medical help and said the explosion was a result of our ammunition somehow. He barely spoke English and we didn't speak any Arabic, so we tried to call the corporal of the guard, who's in charge of all the people on post, and we told him the situation. He told us to make the man and the baby leave.

I have no doubt in my mind that the baby's injuries were a result of coalition forces because all of Iraq is riddled with our unexploded ordnance. Our own training tells us that they use this against us to make roadside bombs, so there's no doubt that it's out there.

After going through the process of boot camp, I was proud of myself and believed I was doing the right thing. They have a way of making you look up to people and they have a way of instilling pride in you. They also joke with you and sing cadences about killing people, and this puts pressure on each individual to be the stereotypical marine, to be ruthless and merciless.

DOMINGO ROSAS

Sergeant, United States Army, Canon Crew member, 3rd Armored Cavalry Regiment

Deployment: April 2003–April 2004, Anbar province

Hometown: Colorado Springs, Colorado

Age at Winter Soldier: 28 years old

We occupied a local train station in an area called al-Qaim near the Syrian border. We called it Tiger Base. I was put in charge of the detainee site, which consisted of a shipping container and a single building surrounded by barbed wire. I had two soldiers to back me up when I was handling the detainees. I was briefed by the sergeant I relieved that the men in the shipping container were captured combatants, and I was to deprive them of sleep. So I had them stand inside the shipping container, face to the walls, no talking. I let them have blankets because it was cold, but they were not allowed to sit or lay down. When they started falling or dozing off, they put their heads on the wall. I was outside the shipping container and just smacked it with a pickax handle to keep them awake. The men in the building were noncombatant detainees being held for questioning. There were ninety-three men, altogether.

Using one of them to translate, I told them that they had a clean slate with me. If they didn't give me any trouble, then the next twenty-four hours would pass calmly. If they did, I told them it would be a long twenty-four hours. I just prayed that they didn't give me any trouble because I didn't know what I would have had to do. They even told me I was a good man while I was in charge of them.

One day a body bag was dropped off to me. When the soldiers came to retrieve it the next morning, they threw it on top of some junk in the back of a truck, but rigor mortis had already set in and it wouldn't fit inside the truck. So the solder started stomping on it, I mean, really stomping it. I couldn't imagine—I was like, "How can you do that?"

I also had a former Iraqi general, Major General Abed Hamed Mow-housh, who was taken from my custody. I was told to keep him separated from the other noncombatants and give him everything he needed: "If he asks for anything, hook him up, take care of him, and don't harass him." I was like, "Well, I don't need somebody to tell me to not harass somebody." A soldier told me later, "Hey, he died during questioning, during his inter-rogation." I thought to myself, "How tough does a question have to be to kill?" I don't know exactly what went on during his interrogation, but he was fine when I had him.

Days after he was taken from my custody, I had his fourteen-year-old son, who was a very bright child and spoke four languages. He was sup-posed to be taken to his father. I was told that would get him to talk a little more. Instead, the boy was being taken to identify his father's body. Now, I'm not sure, but if that child was pro-American or one of our friends and allies, I'm pretty sure he is not an ally of ours anymore.

Sometime later the detainee site was taken over and rebuilt by men called OGAs, which stood for Other Governmental Agency. That's a pretty vague term. They built high walls around the detainee center. I figured, "Well, yeah, they're terrorists. You don't want them seeing out. You want to contain them, deny them any information that they could use to escape." Later on I realized it was also so we couldn't see in.

One night I was told to bring a message down to the detainee site. I knocked on the door, and when they opened it, I witnessed one detainee being kicked around on the ground in the mud, rolled over again and again. The agent was just kicking him with his foot, rolling him over in the mud, pouring water on his face, the whole waterboarding thing. Another detainee was standing there with a bag over his head and was forced to carry a huge rock until he just physically couldn't do it anymore and just collapsed. That image seared itself into my mind's eye, and I can't forget it. I won't forget it…[cries].

As I wrap this up, I just want to say two things. The longer we live as a human race, we're supposed to be getting smarter and wiser and better. To the vets that we're trying to bring home alive, decades from now, when you've got your grandchild sitting on your knee, bouncing in front of you, just try to remember what we did here today, under the flag, IVAW.

Sergeant Domingo Rosas at the conclusion of his testimony.
PHOTO: MIKE HASTIE

GEOFFREY MILLARD

Sergeant, New York Army National Guard,
Combat Engineer, 42nd Infantry Division
Rear Operations Center

Deployment: October 2004–October 2005,
Forward Operating Base Speicher

Hometown: Troy, New York; Washington, D.C.

Age at Winter Soldier: 27 years old

It's no surprise to anyone who's been deployed since September 11 that the word "haji" is used to dehumanize people, not just in Iraq and Afghanistan, but anyone. We bought haji DVDs at haji shops, from the hajis that worked there. The Pakistani KBR employees who did our laundry became hajis. The KBR employees who worked inside our chow halls became hajis. Everyone not in the U.S. forces became a haji: not a person, not a name, a haji.

I used to have conversations with members of my unit, and I would ask them why they used that term, especially members of my unit who are people of color. It used to shock me that they would. Their answers were very similar, almost always. "They're just hajis, who cares?" That came from ranks as low as mine, sergeant, all the way up to a lieutenant colonel in my unit.

The highest-ranking officer that I ever heard use this word was the commanding officer during my deployment to Iraq: General George W. Casey, Jr. At a briefing that my unit, the 42nd Infantry Division Rear Operations Center at FOB Speicher, gave to General Casey, I heard him refer to the Iraqi people as hajis. I've heard several generals, including the 42nd Infantry Division commander, Major General Joseph J. Taluto, and Brigadier General Thomas Sullivan, use these terms in reference to the Iraqi people. These things start at the top, not at the bottom.

I have one story that I want to share with you. One of the most horrifying experiences of my tour, something that still stays with me, was during a briefing I gave.

In the early summer 2005, in the 42nd Infantry Division's area of operations, there was a traffic control point shooting. Traffic control point shootings are rather common in Iraq. They happen on a near-daily basis.

A vehicle was driving quickly toward a traffic control point. A young machine gunner made a split-second decision that the vehicle was a threat and put two hundred .50-caliber machine gun rounds into the vehicle. He killed a mother, a father, and two children. The boy was age four and the girl was age three.

After the officer in charge briefed it to the general, Colonel William Rochelle of the 42nd Infantry Division turned in his chair to the entire division level staff, and said in a very calm manner, "If these fucking hajis learned to drive, this shit wouldn't happen." I looked around the TOC at the other officers, at the other enlisted men. As a sergeant, I think I was the lowest-ranking person in that room. I didn't see any dissenting body language or disagreeing head-nods. Everyone agreed, "If these fucking hajis learned to drive, this shit wouldn't happen."

That stayed with me the rest of my tour. I looked around every time "haji" was used, and I thought about that soldier who will carry that with him for the rest of his life, and I thought about the four Iraqis whose bloodline was ended on that day.

Colonel Rochelle could not think of any of that, but only his own racism and dehumanization that has started at the commander in chief of this war and worked its way down the entire chain of command.

MICHAEL PRYSNER

Corporal, United States Army Reserve, Aerial Intelligence Specialist, 10th Mountain Division, 173rd Airborne Brigade

Deployment: March 2003–February 2004

Hometown: Tampa, Flordia

Age at Winter Soldier: 24 years old

When I first joined the army, I was told that racism no longer existed in the military. A legacy of inequality and discrimination was suddenly washed away by something called the Equal Opportunity Program. We would sit through mandatory classes, and every unit had an EO representative to ensure that no elements of racism could resurface. The army seemed firmly dedicated to smashing any hint of racism.

Then September 11 happened, and I began to hear new words like "towel-head," and "camel jockey," and the most disturbing, "sand nigger." These words did not initially come from my fellow lower-enlisted soldiers, but from my superiors; my platoon sergeant, my first sergeant, my battalion commander. All the way up the chain of command, these viciously racist terms were suddenly acceptable.

When I got to Iraq in 2003, I learned a new word, "haji." Haji was the enemy. Haji was every Iraqi. He was not a person, a father, a teacher, or a worker. It's important to understand where this word came from. To Muslims, the most important thing is to take a pilgrimage to Mecca, the Hajj. Someone who has taken this pilgrimage is a haji. It's something that, in traditional Islam, is the highest calling in the religion. We took the best thing from Islam and made it into the worst thing.

Since the creation of this country, racism has been used to justify expansion and oppression. Native Americans were called "savages," the Africans were called all sorts of things to excuse slavery, and Vietnam veterans know the multitude of words used to justify that imperialist war.

So haji was the word we used. It was the word we used on this particular mission I'm going to talk about. We've heard a lot about raids and kicking down the doors of people's houses and ransacking their houses, but this was a different kind of raid.

We never got any explanation for our orders. We were only told that a group of five or six houses was now property of the U.S. military, and we had to go in and make those families leave their houses.

We went to these houses and informed the families that their homes were no longer theirs. We provided them no alternative, nowhere to go, no compensation. They were very confused and very scared. They did not know what to do and would not leave, so we had to remove them.

One family in particular, a woman with two small girls, a very elderly man, and two middle-aged men; we dragged them from their house and threw them onto the street. We arrested the men because they refused to leave, and we sent them off to prison.

A few months later I found out, as we were short interrogators and I was given that assignment. I oversaw and participated in hundreds of interrogations. I remember one in particular that I'm going to share with you. It was the moment that really showed me the nature of this occupation.

This particular detainee was already stripped down to his underwear, hands behind his back and a sandbag on his head. I never saw this man's face. My job was to take a metal folding chair and smash it against the wall next to his head—he was faced against the wall with his nose touching it—while a fellow soldier screamed the same question over and over again. No matter what his answer, my job was to slam the chair against the wall. We did this until we got tired.

I was told to make sure he kept standing up, but something was wrong with his leg. He was injured, and he kept falling to the ground. The sergeant in charge would come and tell me to get him up on his feet, so I'd have to pick him up and put him against the wall. He kept going down. I kept pulling him up and putting him against the wall. My sergeant was upset with me for not making him continue to stand. He picked him up and slammed him against the wall several times. Then he left. When the man went down on the ground again, I noticed blood pouring down from under the sandbag. I let him sit, and when I noticed my sergeant coming again, I would tell him quickly to stand up.

Instead of guarding my unit from this detainee, I realized I was guarding the detainee from my unit.

I tried hard to be proud of my service, but all I could feel was shame. Racism could no longer mask the reality of the occupation. These are human beings. I've since been plagued by guilt. I feel guilt anytime I see an elderly man, like the one who couldn't walk who we rolled onto a stretcher and told the Iraqi police to take him away. I feel guilt anytime I see a mother with her children, like the one who cried hysterically and screamed that we were worse than Saddam as we forced her from her home. I feel guilt anytime I see a young girl, like the one I grabbed by the arm and dragged into the street.

We were told we were fighting terrorists; the real terrorist was me, and the real terrorism is this occupation. Racism within the military has long been an important tool to justify the destruction and occupation of another country. Without racism, soldiers would realize that they have more in common with the Iraqi people than they do with the billionaires who send us to war.

I threw families onto the street in Iraq, only to come home and find families thrown onto the street in this country, in this tragic and unnecessary foreclosure crisis. Our enemies are not five thousand miles away, they are right here at home, and if we organize and fight, we can stop this war, we can stop this government, and we can create a better world.

CIVILIAN TESTIMONY: THE COST OF WAR IN IRAQ

Journalist and computer programmer Salam Talib is one of the few Iraqis permitted to come to the United States.

·PHOTO: MIKE HASTIE

INTRODUCTION

Over the past five years, U.S. military raids, patrols, and bombings have taken a terrible toll on the Iraqi people. Already straining before the war under dual weights of international sanctions and Saddam Hussein's brutal dictatorship, Iraqi society now finds itself in nearly complete collapse.

The cycle of violence that began with the U.S. invasion now permeates every aspect of society. "The humanitarian situation in most of the country remains among the most critical in the world," the International Committee of the Red Cross reported in March 2008. "Because of the conflict, millions of Iraqis have insufficient access to clean water, sanitation and health care.... Civilians continue to be killed in the hostilities. The injured often do not receive adequate medical care. Millions of people have been forced to rely on insufficient supplies of poor-quality water as water and sewage systems suffer from a lack of maintenance and a shortage of engineers."[1] More than five million Iraqis—20 percent of the country's entire population—have fled their homes since the U.S. invasion in 2003. One and a half million Iraqis now live in Syria, while over a million refugees have gone to Jordan, Iran, Egypt, Lebanon, Turkey, and the Gulf States.[2]

The daily reality of living in U.S.-occupied Iraq is so grim it's beyond the comprehension of most Americans. Imagine for a moment that you are the parent of an Iraqi child. Imagine every day when you send your daughter off to school you worry that she could be killed by a car bomb, kidnapped for ransom by a criminal gang, accidentally shot by U.S. troops or neighborhood militias, or simply run over by an American convoy that had been ordered not to stop for "bumps in the road."

Now imagine further that when your daughter gets to school, the school is only half full. Some of your daughter's classmates have been killed and the parents of some of her other classmates pulled them out of school to make sure they don't meet the same fate. In addition, many of the teachers have abandoned their jobs, fleeing the city for the perceived safety of their ancestral farm or the security of a neighboring country. You think every day about following suit—about ditching everything you have and leaving the country—but after five years of war, Syria and Jordan have closed their borders to all but the wealthiest Iraqis. So you continue the only way you know how, dropping your daughter off at school, hoping she'll come home safe, and praying to God that the situation changes.

On television, George Bush, John McCain, David Petraeus, and other prominent Americans talk about "progress" brought on by a "surge" in the number of U.S. troops in Iraq, but this "progress" is not apparent to most Iraqis. A March 2008 ABC/*BBC News* poll showed—by a more than two-to-one margin—that Iraqis believe the "presence of U.S. forces in Iraq" has made the security situation worse rather than better. The same poll showed 72 percent of Iraqis oppose the continued presence of coalition forces in their country. A majority believes the recent troop "surge" has worsened conditions rather than improving them.[3]

More American troops in Iraq has also brought more raids and sent a record number of Iraqis to prison—so many that Saddam Hussein's old lockups cannot hold all those America has incarcerated. The U.S. military has responded by building new prison camps, the largest of which, Camp Bucca, will soon be able to hold thirty thousand detainees. By May 2008 the United States held more than twenty-four thousand "security detainees" in Iraq—prisoners who are held indefinitely without an arrest warrant, without charge, and with no opportunity for those held to defend themselves in a trial.[4]

Iraqis, like the veterans who spoke at Winter Soldier, clearly see American soldiers as the center of the violence rather than the solution. Wherever the Americans go they are attacked and when they are attacked they return fire. After a while, it hardly matters whether the stray bullet that killed your brother came from an American, an Iraqi, or an al-Qaeda in

Iraq fighter. The point is that if the Americans had never driven their Humvees down your street, your brother would still be alive today.

A Note on the Testimony to Follow:

Members of Iraq Veterans Against the War wanted to bring a full panel of Iraqi civilians to Silver Spring, Maryland to testify at Winter Soldier. However, the Bush administration has largely refused to grant Iraqis visas to come to the United States. As a result, only two Iraqis civilians were able to speak in person at Winter Soldier, one of whose testimony is represented here. So the veterans worked with a team of independent filmmakers who gathered first-person testimony from Iraqis living in Baghdad and Basra as well as from Iraqi refugees who had fled to Jordan and Syria and presented them on giant video screens during Winter Soldier at the National Labor College. Most of the testimony that follows comes from translated excerpts from those videos.

HUDA JABBAR MOHAMMED ALI
Born in 1968
Resident of al-Nidhal District, Baghdad

My husband Amr Abd al-Wahab Abd al-Fatah was killed by the occupation forces. He was forty years old. I have five children. It happened on al-Sa'adoon Street in the al-Nidhal area. On August 8, 2006, at 11 a.m.

My husband was a security guard at a school. When he was killed he was on an official assignment to see the principal's assistant. He was in a car with my brother's wife, my brother, and my brother's wife's uncle who was driving. While he was on the way to our neighborhood, the occupation forces were leaving the area. They were driving fast and firing randomly and my husband got shot in the head. My brother was injured.

I don't understand what happened, because there was no explosion in the area. The American forces were just shooting at everyone in front of them. They didn't want anyone else driving on the road, so they just started shooting everyone, telling them to get out of the way. They shot everyone in front of them. So my husband got killed. Six other people were also killed.

Many members of the neighborhood witnessed this, and when they saw this accident they hurried to it and saw my brother's wife screaming. Ambulances showed up and my husband was rushed to the hospital. Because he had been shot in the head he was completely paralyzed. They rushed him to the operating room but couldn't save his life.

After the incident, I went to a place where the American forces are stationed behind al-Sha'ab Stadium. One of the soldiers there helped me write a letter, which I took to the Green Zone in the hopes that I would be able to get compensation for my loss. They kept sending me from one place to another and I never got any compensation. Now I am supporting my family with the help of God. I work in the school cleaning and assisting but the salary is not enough so I also sell candies in the school. I take care of my five children on my own.

ZAHARA ABBAS
Mother
Iraqi Refugee Living in Syria

It was almost one in the morning. Zainab and I were awake. Everyone else was asleep. We heard airplanes far away, then closer. Then we heard the sounds of tanks in the street. We turned off the TV and we went to sleep.

All of the sudden, my bedroom windows broke. So we ran into the living room and the windows there broke. So we ran into the kitchen and the windows broke.

The freezer moved across the kitchen with such force. The refrigerator doors opened. The tiles fell off the wall. I went back into the living room and all of the sudden I saw American soldiers. There was chaos in the house. We didn't know where to go.

They started shooting at the walls. They even shot the fish tank. It was a dark night for us. They started to search everything. They threw things from the cabinets, they messed up the house. They shot at the doors, the bathroom, at Ahmed's bedroom; there are still traces of the shots.

And I want you to focus on this moment: I'll remember it for the rest of my life. They were taking things, and my daughter Zamzam had been studying for her mid-year exams, and her books were on the floor when she went to bed. They started taking her books and putting them into a bag.

I asked my son, Ali, to ask them to leave the books, they were French lesson books. Ali asked them not to take the books, that they belonged to a student. They hit Ali on the head. They hit him so hard his neck almost broke.

There was a lot of destruction in the house. We had to spend about $8,000 to rebuild the house: the doors, the floor. It's not so much the money as the psychological suffering that we endured and are still enduring. When I think of the raid, it was misery. It had a deep psychological effect. We always remember that night. I still remember my daughter Sarah screaming. She kept screaming and crying. It still affects her.

We took her outside while they were working on fixing our house. When she hears a noise she screams: "The Americans! The Americans are coming!" The girl gets scared.

After they tried and tried to enter the city, and failed,

MOHAMMED AMR
Resident of Adhamiya District, Baghdad

In March 2005 I witnessed the intentional mutilation of corpses by coalition forces. There were seven young men fighting U.S. forces, shooting at them with mortars. On that day the Americans prepared a trap for them because they shot at them from the same place repeatedly. So they captured and killed them.

I saw them when they received the corpses in the Adhamiya police station and they were mutilated. It was an after-death mutilation. They had been stabbed and stabbed again. Their delivery to the police station was very fast. They were killed at 11 a.m. and we received them at 1 p.m. So it's impossible to be done by others.

Once they attacked our house to arrest my little brother. The raid started on April 4, 2007, at 2:30 a.m. and lasted until 5 a.m. They attacked us in a very stressful way. They exploded the outer door with two bombs. Our wives and children were in bed, and we too were scared. They captured me, my father, and my brother, they wrapped our hands so tight my hands turned blue. And they dislocated my shoulder. They beat my father too and he's sixty years old. Then they started to beat us, accusing us of weapons possession, calling us terrorists, and they took away my brother and went away.

The target was my little brother. When the accuser pointed at him, they started beating him until blood came out of his face and every part of his body. They didn't find any weapons, not even a bullet, but my mother was holding a little bag containing all our possessions, worth about $13,000. The interpreter took it and gave it to the American soldiers. They also took our cell phones, our blankets, even our clothes. They stayed for almost three hours.

My parents speak excellent English and they told the commanding officer that it was our money they were taking. He answered, "Choose between your money and your honor," so we bought our honor with our money! We didn't see any humanity in the American soldiers, only cruelty.

SHAYMA
Student, 11 years old
Resident of Adhamiya District, Baghdad

One day I was in school in the morning. We were in class. All of a sudden, American soldiers came in and asked us to leave. They spent about half of the school day. More than two hours.

They said there were weapons or terrorists in the school. So they asked us to go outside. They started searching and turned the entire school upside down. They searched the classrooms, the teachers' rooms, the principal's office. I was in fifth grade. We were terrified.

They said we had weapons and hid them. And that we had materials like explosives. They thought the school had them, but I haven't seen anything like that and they didn't find anything. When they left, they didn't apologize to the teachers or the principal. They came quickly and left quickly. We were really scared. I was with my sister and we both closed our eyes.

They should not behave that way. We were children. They should have at least come in using another way other than coming with machine guns drawn. If they had to come in, they should have come in a normal way, maybe tell us first that this is what they need to do, maybe come after school to search it, tell us that they were concerned about our lives. And not in the middle of the school day and we were all scared from their weapons.

After the raid, we left the school quickly. We left our books and bags. We were frightened. We didn't care about our bags. Our parents were waiting for us outside the house because they saw American soldiers and tanks. So they were waiting for us.

After that, my mother and father decided I should quit school. I was very disturbed and sad by that. They had to because of the deteriorated security situation. No safety. The American soldiers suddenly come to school. The militias suddenly come in. Most of my friends and classmates made the same decision and stopped going to school after that. Half the teachers also stayed at home, concerned about their lives. The other half continued to come to school but not regularly.

I am very ambitious. And did very well in school, but alas I couldn't achieve my dream because of the security situation in Baghdad and the killing and violence and terrorism. I always wanted to be a good citizen for my society and achieve at least one of my dreams that I have been dreaming of. I wanted to achieve the Iraqi children's dreams, children who faced the same tragedy as mine and my classmates at school. Now I am afraid of everything. Now any incident happens in front of me, I start crying and get frightened. I am sure it is not only me who feels this way; many Iraqis have been feeling the same.

I wish for every Iraqi as well as me and other kids my age and older to achieve their dreams. And for the violence to disappear. I wish for Iraq to be better than this, so that at least we, the new generation, can freely study and learn in order to build a better society, fix this destruction, end the violence in our country, and make our country beautiful. We want to be good people for our society to build our civilization not in a case of terror and fear and destruction and see all these things that affect everybody. Not just me or my sister or few people, I am talking about everybody who lives in Iraq.

SALAM TALIB
Journalist and Computer Engineer
32 years old
Resident of Baghdad

S hukran jazeelan lehadhurikum wa insh'Allah nethheb jamea'n ile al-Iraq wa nettasharek fi el-sa'ade wa aman. Al-yom sanattahdeth an al-wada' fi al-Iraq.[5] [stunned silence from the audience of veterans]

I'm sorry—did I speak in Arabic? Guys—I think this is the problem. Iraqis actually speak another language.

I worked with most of the independent journalists that came to Iraq. I didn't work for big corporations. Before the American invasion, I was a computer engineer. I came from a family that had been oppressed by Saddam. After Saddam was overthrown, I worked as a journalist just because there was nothing else to do.

One day I was driving in Baghdad, crossing an American checkpoint, and I was stopped along with all the other people. That day I was grouchy because the electricity had been off all day the day before. Before the war, when there was no electricity we used to sleep outside on the roof, but we can't do that now. It's not safe, because you never know what's going to fall on you.

So I had to sleep indoors and it was really hot. And at seven in the morning I had to go to work. So what happened—at this checkpoint—they stopped me. And as you all notice I use crutches, because I had polio as a baby. One of the soldiers came to me, pointing a gun at me and said, "Get out of the car." But he wasn't saying it in polite, nice language, he was swearing and I began to fear for my safety. But despite the risk, I decided to speak my own language, a language the soldier didn't understand.

I put my hands up and I waited. I knew if I grabbed the crutches he would shoot me before he realized that they were crutches and not a weapon. An apology would have done nothing for me. So I decided to just sit there until he opened the door.

He continued shouting at me and when the other soldiers heard him shouting the translator came. There were about fifty soldiers and one translator. And translators in Iraq, they got paid about—about ten to fifteen dollars a day at a time. The rate is still less than forty dollars a month. So these translators are not the best. And who wants to work this kind of job anyway? You are a moving target for people who hate the Americans. After work, you go home to your family in a civilian neighborhood and the soldiers go home to their base. There is no way to do it.

So the translator came and he didn't know the word for disabled. So he translated as best he could—he looked at the car and he looked at my crutches inside—and then he said, "Oh, he's injured in his leg."

When the soldiers heard that, they assumed I had been injured in a firefight. One of the soldiers threw open the door and grabbed me out of the car, put me on the ground, put the gun over me, and started swearing at me saying, "Where did you get injured?"

And then I decided, "I think it's time to speak English." So I spoke with them in English and he was like, "Man, why you didn't say that from the beginning?"

After this event, I knew that any contact with U.S. soldiers could be deadly. I have seen it happen to many other people. Many of my friends have been shot accidentally. I began counting my friends—how many of them have died since the start of this occupation. But after I got to thirty-four I decided to stop because I could never catch up. There's always another death, and then another.

I want to tell you about another incident. I was driving one night, around 9 p.m., which is very late in Iraq. I was on the highway just by myself driving really crazy because I wanted to get home before I ran into any soldiers or the people who were trying to kill them.

And there was a voice in my head saying "This is very dangerous." There were no other cars around. Then I looked in my rearview mirror and there was another car—a white pickup truck behind me. And the guy who was driving it, he looked like a farmer or something. So I decided that I would let him go in front of me so if something happened to him, I would know there was danger ahead.

I felt bad about it afterward, but....

So this farmer was driving about a hundred meters in front of me—and I saw these three tanks. They were in the middle of the empty highway. And these tanks had no lights, no sign—nothing.

And there were about thirty soldiers and they were lying on the ground in a shooting position. And I didn't see them at first, I saw them after they saw our lights and the cars coming. They turned on one of the tank's lights and I was wondering, "Is that a tank? Is it something else?"

So I decided to slow down. And then on the loudspeaker they said, in English, "Stop—deadly force is gonna be used." I heard that and I understand English so I stopped right away. But the other car, he didn't understand and went right through them. And then I heard—I heard them shoot him. They shot him and I felt like I killed him—I put him in front of me. That should have been me. Should be me.

I was just stopped there, watching them, just frozen there. And I saw them drag him out of the truck. I watched the American soldiers pull the canvas cover off the bed of his pickup. They looked inside the bed and it was just vegetables. It was lettuce—lots of lettuce. And I wondered to myself, "Wow—you could be killed for transporting lettuce in this country."

In December 2004 my friend was killed in my car because the killers thought he was me. So I decided that was gonna be my last day in Iraq.

For all the people who talk about progress in Iraq, who think the American military should stay in Iraq, I have a simple question: "What about you going to Iraq?" I will buy your ticket. You go and enjoy your time in Iraq. If you think it's great, go there—stay there. I will let you stay in the house I left behind. The Americans have a base right across the street from it. They have ten snipers just pointing at my house and my neighbors' homes.

I don't know how many of you have seen Iraqis except the soldiers. But actually Iraqis are human beings–they are like you. They have families. They have friends. And actually they have bigger families than you.

My family is five brothers and five sisters. We are eleven. I stopped counting how many nieces and nephews that I have. I think I have fifty-three. And all of this from one mother and one father.

I really respect those soldiers that are the ones that don't want to deploy again, and the soldiers that left the military when they noticed what they were doing and what they should do. I really think they're heroes.

Here at Winter Soldier, I have had the opportunity to speak with many veterans and have really enjoyed it. I wish I had met them back home in Iraq. But many of them told me, "No, you didn't want to see us there." Over there, it would have been combat, but now we are talking human to human.

Today, I think if these veterans saw me back over there in the same situation, they would never shoot me. They're the same people, but they've realized that I'm a human just like them, and actually speak the same language. So I think if the language is a problem, today I'm gonna teach you all Arabic. That's what I'm gonna do.

And I'm gonna start teaching you the words that we should all learn. The first word you should learn is my name. My name is Salam—it means "peace." So this word—you should learn it. And if all Americans learned this word, I think they will never, ever go to other people and steal their peace.

DIVIDE AND CONQUER: GENDER AND SEXUALITY IN THE MILITARY

Margaret Stevens was called up to defend Ground Zero after 9/11 as a member of the New Jersey National Guard.

PHOTO: MIKE HASTIE

INTRODUCTION

Dehumanization bred through training and combat stress not only leads to brutality against the "enemy," it also leads to discrimination and brutality within the ranks. Women, gays and lesbians, and heterosexual men perceived as "weak" are often targeted.

The large numbers of female soldiers on the battlefields is one of the key differences between the Iraq War and previous conflicts. More than 160,000 female soldiers have been deployed to Iraq and Afghanistan, compared with the 7,500 women who served in Vietnam and the 41,000 who were dispatched to the Gulf War in the early '90s.[1] Today, women make up 15 percent of U.S. active-duty forces and 11 percent of soldiers deployed to the front.[2] These women, who are already risking their lives in misguided occupations, must often fight a second battle against servicemembers wearing the same uniform. Nearly a third of female veterans say they were sexually assaulted or raped while in the military, and 71 percent to 90 percent say they were sexually harassed by the men with whom they served.[3]

In the testimony that follows, these soldiers describe how the chill and pain of sexual assault followed them through basic training and into the conflict zone. Comprehensive statistics on the sexual assault of female soldiers in Iraq have not been collected, but early numbers revealed a problem so bad that in 2004 former Defense Secretary Donald Rumsfeld ordered a task force to investigate.[4] The investigation did not result in any prosecutions, but rather in a new website to clarify that sexual assault is illegal.

Regular classes on sexual assault and harassment were also initiated, but many servicemembers do not take them seriously.

When a rape or sexual assault occurs within the military, reporting it is intrinsically difficult. Such incidents usually occur in a setting where the victim lives and works. In most cases, this means that victims must continue to live and work closely with their perpetrators, often leading to increased feelings of helplessness, powerlessness, and being at risk for further victimization. It is usually impossible to remain anonymous. Often the victim must rely on the perpetrator (or associates of the perpetrator) to approve or provide medical and psychological care. "Perpetrators are frequently peers or supervisors responsible for making decisions about work-related evaluations and promotions," notes the VA's National Center for Post-Traumatic Stress Disorder. "In addition, victims are often forced to choose between continuing military careers during which they are forced to have frequent contact with their perpetrators or sacrificing their career goals in order to protect themselves from future victimization."[5]

If heterosexual women face barriers in reporting discrimination within the military, the situation is even worse for gay men and lesbians. Gay and lesbian Americans are increasingly accepted in civilian society and (at present) allowed to marry in California and Massachusetts, but are not allowed to serve openly in the Armed Forces. If a gay soldier reports abuse to his or her chain of command, the servicemember can be immediately expelled from the military for violating the Pentagon's "Don't Ask, Don't Tell" policy. Over eleven thousand servicemembers have been expelled since President Bill Clinton implemented the policy in 1994.[5]

Military leaders have stuck by this discriminatory policy even as they have loosened recruiting standards for everyone else. In 2006 an estimated one in five soldiers being recruited to fight in Iraq received a "moral waiver" in order to enter the service. From 2003 to 2006 the military allowed 106,000 people to enter with troubled histories, including 4,230 convicted felons, 43,977 individuals convicted of serious misdemeanors such as assault, and 58,561 convicted illegal drug offenders.[7] In the army, allowable offenses include making terrorist threats, murder, and kidnapping.[8]

Why, veterans at Winter Soldier asked, does the Pentagon allow kidnappers and murderers to join the military, but not openly gay men and lesbians? Consider this question as you read their testimony on "Gender and Sexuality in the Military."

JEN HOGG

Sergeant, New York Army National Guard, Track Mechanic

Deployments: Ground Zero after 9/11

Hometown: Buffalo, New York

Age at Winter Soldier: 26 years old

I attended basic training in 2000 and went through Advanced Individual Training (AIT) from November 29, 2000, until March 1, 2001. During AIT, after the Supreme Court ended the Florida recount in *Bush v. Gore*, a male E7 teacher, during his introduction of the class for that day, stated that he was glad that Bush was going to be president because now we won't have all these fags in the army.

I did not report the incident because I felt it would single me out and cause repercussions. I felt as though I would easily fit the stereotype of a lesbian physically and I was in a specialty that was heavily male. I heard the word "fag" used on a daily basis by other soldiers while in uniform. In basic training I helped a straight soldier report to our drill sergeant another female recruit constantly calling her a "dyke" due mostly to what I suspect was her short hair. The woman had a boyfriend at home so I felt helping her to report the name-calling was safe for her and necessary because the label "dyke" can cause someone to be kicked out of the military. I believe the drill sergeant told the offending woman to "cut it out." The incident later in AIT did not hold the same level of safety, as I was vulnerable both as a lesbian myself and as a lower rank of the E7.

For myself harassment meant verbal harassment. When I removed my battle dress uniform top in hot environments I would often hear a comment about my body such as "where you been hiding them puppies" in reference to my breasts. Since I generally liked the soldier who said it I said nothing to him, not wanting to ruin our working relationship.

Male soldiers also tried to do my job for me. I was the smallest soldier and would have male soldiers politely take a wrench from me and do the job I was preparing to do. While they did so as a gesture of being nice, it gave the impression that women are weak and unable to do their jobs. Many times I had to argue politely to let me do my job and if they wanted to help me out I would be sure to ask for it in the case something proved beyond my capacity. On the flip side of that, being smaller allowed me to access to certain areas larger males could not. I felt capable as a mechanic even if my physical strength did not always match the larger males, something I made up for in devising ways to use my brain instead of strength alone.

There was at one time a clock in the shop with a photo of a topless woman. Instead of reporting it as a workplace violation I just took care of the problem myself by applying a healthy coating of Never-Seez grease as a bikini top.

We were expected to clean up in the bathrooms of the shop. In the women's room there was not proper soap for cleaning automotive dirt from one's hands. I had to knock on the men's room and use their soap and washbasin. It took nearly three years to get usable soap. At the time I was the only female mechanic but there was a few other women who also used that bathroom, such as supply and armorers. The women's room itself was not a safe haven for women, though, as men often used that bathroom when they wanted to take a shit, as it were. When a male was in my bathroom I had to go all the way to the front of our armory or just wait outside and give the male dirty looks on his way out.

In my unit all briefings relating to sexism were treated as a joke and never attended by all members of the unit as most people found ways to avoid briefings in general or have a friend sign them in even if they were not present. Briefings on sexual orientation—"Don't Ask, Don't Tell"— were treated as through the briefer was embarrassed to give them. In both cases the briefing was not given in a serious manner.

Being a member of the National Guard and lesbian on 9/11 is what initially led me to begin to question my involvement in the military and the military's involvement in the world. If on 9/11 I did not have the freedom to hug my girlfriend goodbye before we left as a unit for New York City then what freedom was I protecting? What freedom could we offer to the world if we treat it so restrictively based on who a person falls in love with?

I had one friend in the Guard in another company of my unit (Geoff Millard) who knew of my sexuality so we always hung out. This caused the rumor that I was a dominatrix and that Geoff and I were sleeping together. I let that exist due to the safety net of heterosexuality it offered. In the military men and women are nearly never allowed to be just friends, they are almost always assumed to be "fucking." In reality in my experience most people breaking military regulations in regards to sexual regulations are straight. I saw multiple instances of adultery between fellow soldiers who had husbands and wives at home.

Before I joined the military I was out in high school and was often known as the gay girl in a very positive way, despite being in the South. After I left the military in 2005 I continued to censor myself in regards to me being a lesbian and only recently have begun to speak out publicly about it. While I never hid my sexuality after leaving the military, I rarely went out of my way in new situations to mention it. It has been very liberating to begin to break that lasting effect of my military career. I also have felt poorly about my response to being in a position to help learn with and educate men and women about the power and effects of sexism. It wasn't until after I left the military I fully learned about this myself and have vowed to not make the same mistakes in IVAW or life in general.

ABBY HISER

Sergeant, Wisconsin Army National Guard,
Heavy Construction Equipment Operator

Deployments: August 2003–April 2004,
Talil Air Base, near Nasiriyah

Hometown: Rice Lake, Wisconsin

Age at Winter Soldier: 26 years old

I have many thoughts and feelings on my service, some positive, some negative, and some indifferent. Yet, as a female in the military, I have encountered my fair share of inappropriate, unprofessional, and discriminatory acts.

I'm a friendly and confident person; I like to make friends and talk with others. Shortly after I joined I started to make friends, but my friendliness was misinterpreted as promiscuity. There were false rumors of me sleeping with a married man. I learned my lesson, and I kept to myself. But then I was labeled as rude, mean, snooty, or a witch or the "B-word." I joined the military to defend my country and not my integrity and self-worth.

There needs to be more respect and professionalism in the training field. I was disrespected by an ROTC soldier during a summer assignment when he inappropriately patted me down during a training exercise. I was playing a role of the enemy, and he grabbed my chest with both hands and patted me down inappropriately, and he walked away laughing like it was a joke. He just laughed with his buddies, like, "Oh, look at her, she really enjoyed that." Like it was no problem. This happens more than you think and it needs to be addressed.

I was assigned to an engineering unit as a heavy equipment operator. When it came to assigning equipment, my sergeant stated that he was going to advocate for me to be assigned as an excavator because I showed skill and confidence. My sergeant was a civilian excavator operator as well, so coming from him this was quite a compliment. Still, I did not get my promised equipment. My sergeant was told he was only advocating for me because he had a crush on me. This led me to think one of two things: Did he really have a crush on me and I wasn't a good operator? Or do the higher-ranking NCOs not believe that a woman could be as good as this experienced operator reports?

Just shy of three years in the service, I was selected to go to Primary Leadership Development Course (PLDC), sergeant leadership training. I had worked very hard to get this opportunity. I even left college mid-semester for two weeks to attend. I was under the assumption that I'd be promoted as soon as the sergeant slot opened up. Shortly after completing the course, I volunteered to go to Iraq early and deployed with a unit that was not my own.

While sitting in the desert, I filled out the paperwork to be promoted and I sent it in, only to find out that I couldn't be promoted while deployed with another unit. However, it was okay for them to promote a male sergeant who had barely been in our unit for six months and had volunteered to go to Iraq as I did.

Once I came back, I resubmitted the paperwork for the promotion once again. I was finally promoted in October 2005, three years after completing PLDC. Once I was in a leadership position, it was difficult to gain the respect I deserved. On my last mission, I was the only female. The mission became difficult after I reminded a lower-ranked male soldier what appropriate conduct was when speaking to a sergeant; he did not respond well, and the rest of the mission was difficult.

When I was deployed in Iraq with another unit, I was one of four women in the company. We all felt our section leader had some sort of resentment toward us. There were many opportunities to assist other units, platoons with missions going outside the wire. I mentioned I wanted to join a few of these missions, yet I was immediately turned down due to my lack of time in Iraq. Yet there were men there just as long as I was or less, and they were allowed to go on these missions, so I really don't understand how that worked. He did, however, make a nice attempt to even the playing field when he volunteered me to do patrolling with other platoons on Sunday, and Sunday was our only day off.

Overall, I've learned how to overcome and succeed in the military despite the unnecessary obstacles. I feel women in the military should be judged on an individual basis on performance alone. The stereotyping and the blatant disregard of the many issues we must deal with must end, no matter how large or small the issue. We work among men doing just as men do. We deserve the same respect.

PATRICIA McCANN
Specialist, Illinois Army National Guard, MSE Systems Operator

Deployments: May 2003–2004, Baghdad International Airport

Hometown: Chicago, Illinois

Age at Winter Soldier: 25 years old

I enlisted in the Illinois National Guard when I was seventeen. It's hard to be a veteran of the war and a woman because I feel a lot of the time my experience gets boiled down to what I experience as a woman, and I don't get to talk about some of the things that I experienced as a soldier. But I'm gonna keep it to the issues of sexism, homophobia, and racism today, which I think are tools that we use to justify our degrading behavior toward the other, the enemy.

In this process of dehumanization, every veteran knows the first person to become dehumanized is the soldier themselves. They're all used from day one to break people down. I mean, if my mother only knew that I would be hearing drill sergeants say to males right next to me in basic training, "Does your 'P-word' hurt? Do you need a tampon?" If my mother only knew.

I'm gonna talk more about how encompassing and pervasive the sexist climate was during my tour in Iraq. In my unit, rank structure was used to coerce women into sexual relationships. The incident that set the tone for the whole deployment took place while we were still stateside, waiting to go to the Middle East in Fort Riley, Kansas. We were told in class that according to the Rules of Engagement we should shoot anyone that we felt threatened by. We were told that we should be threatened by men and women because they could be hiding explosives under their long black robes and burkas. We should be threatened by pregnant women because it probably wasn't a baby they had in their belly but explosives. We should be threatened by children because they were used as bait to lure us into situations. I felt that all the things they told us were used as tools to either emasculate the male enemies or condemn femininity as evil and dangerous.

While we were having this class outside, one of our platoon sergeants was watching us from his room window, and he took pictures of all the young females and later taped them to our door, really creepy pictures. When I tried to complain about this, I was told he didn't hurt us, nothing was wrong. Over time, we heard this again and again, "He's not hurting you. You can't complain about this. He's married." There's always this idea that you're gonna ruin someone's career if you talk about stuff.

Another incident I'd like to talk about was on Christmas Day 2003. I was at Baghdad International Airport and a CID officer was drunk, stumbling around our company area. He had a cup of vodka—I found him in this storage room on the side of our building alone, and he flashed me his badge. I just was like, "Why are you showing me your badge?" And he asked me, "Who can I fuck who will suck my dick?"

And at this point, I just was really just like, "Get outta here," you know— "Just leave." We tried to get rid of him, but he was the guest of a woman who was put into our company. We asked this woman to make him leave and thought he left, but apparently he didn't. The next time we saw him, he was bleeding from his hand, and the story that we heard was that he cocked his gun and somehow caught his hand in it. I don't know how he cut his hand, but that night there was a big investigation.

I want to read this memo to commanders in MEDCOM, Regional Medical Commands, and the subject is Military Treatment Management of Reported Alleged Sexual Assault Cases, Payment for Exams and Kits: "SAD kits"—SAD kits, which are rape kits—"are not included in TRICARE coverage. The Assistant Secretary of Defense is soliciting legislative changes to TRICARE benefit which will include these kits within covered TRICARE supplies. Until that occurs, beneficiaries may be liable for bills for these supplies. Some states may have victim assistance compensation programs which will pay for certain accommodations for victims of sexual assaults, including S-A-D kits."

That's how the military takes care of rape victims.

This is important not just because of what happens to people in the military. Think about Abu Ghraib, I mean, think about the way sexual objectification manifests itself and that's what happening in Iraq to Iraqis, and it's disgusting.

WENDY BARRANCO
Specialist, United States Army Reserve,
Medic
Deployments: September 2005–June 2006
Tikrit
Hometown: Los Angeles, California
Age at Winter Soldier: 22 years old

I joined straight out of high school. I was seventeen. My first experience with sexual harassment was with my recruiter. He was married and his wife was pregnant, and he used to make it a requirement for me to go with him and talk to other soldiers about joining the army in order to reel them in. One night he got drunk, and he had to stay at a hotel because his wife was mad at him. I drove him to the hotel and then he came on to me; I was able to weasel my way out of it and get out. That was my first brush with just the military and sexual harassment.

When I was in basic training, we heard stories of drill sergeants sleeping with trainees. When I deployed I worked in a clinic. I was a combat medic and had this interest in looking at gruesome things. I asked one of the surgeons there if there was a way I could go to the operating room and watch a case. He said, "OK," and the next day he asked if I wanted to start working there.

I agreed and started the next day at seven in the morning, and through that whole deployment, I was harassed like every single day. I dreaded every day I went to work because this surgeon would catch me alone in a hallway and push himself against me with his hands behind his back. It's extremely difficult to do your job proficiently, efficiently, and correctly when you have to look out for one of your own supervisors.

So basically what he was practicing was quid quo pro, you know, "I transferred you to the operating room, so therefore, you need to give me something back." This person was in an extremely important position and he had transferred me over. All I kept thinking was, "If I speak out, it's gonna be my word against him, and I'm just a specialist, so who are they gonna believe? Are they gonna get rid of the guy that's making all the decisions and saving lives or me, the disposable specialist?" It never got to a physical point because he knew exactly what he was doing, and I never reported it because I knew the command wouldn't do anything about it. It's not easy to speak up— you're looked at as a snitch for turning around and talking about your brothers and sisters and comrades that you're working with day in and day out.

Some people point out that we do sexual harassment training. We do consideration-of-others training, but the type of training that goes on is check-the-box training. Which usually consists of an NCO in the front of a room giving a PowerPoint presentation and then we're done, everybody goes home.

It's really hard for me to sit here and kind of tell you all this because I joined trying to be patriotic. I joined to try to do something for my country, and the last thing I would've imagined would have been joining an organization where I would be harassed this way by my own peers, by my own comrades.

ANONYMOUS
United States Coast Guard, Burlington,
Vermont

I began my duty at United States Coast Guard Station, Burlington, Vermont, on February 2, 2006. I was one of two females assigned to the base of around twenty-five Coast Guard members. On an almost daily basis I would hear comments based on my gender. One person told me females should never have been allowed to join the Coast Guard. A third class petty officer told me to go to the galley to mess cook because women belong in the kitchen. I was also told by a member of my command that I am not capable of doing certain things like being on an ice crew because I am a female and those jobs are for men.

While in the lounge watching TV with my shipmates a male seaman came and beat me with a rolled-up newspaper. No one tried to stop it and a few of my shipmates just sat there and laughed. I was upset and surprised and didn't want things to escalate so I moved to my barrack room. The next day the chief and his second-in-command, the executive petty officer (XPO), found out what happened and I was called into the chief's office where they told me that they were worried I would not be able to deal with pulling a floater from the water because I was weak. They told me I made a mistake by joining the Coast Guard and that I would need to get a psychologist's evaluation. Our base was small and didn't have any medical facilities, so they sent me to the Integrated Support Command Center in Boston.

I spent a few days in Boston and was then sent on to New London, Connecticut to meet with the psychologist at the Coast Guard Academy. His advice to me—ignore what my shipmates were doing, "sailors will be sailors." He said their behavior was acceptable, cleared me, and allowed me to go back to Burlington.

While I was on base in Burlington many of my shipmates warned me that one of the male seamen was an abnormal character and advised me not to be friends with him. Due to my open mind and desire to be liked and get to know all my shipmates, I decided to befriend him anyways and gained his trust—we spoke often.

On May 30, 2006, the seaman called me and asked if I wanted to go for a drive. I was not doing anything so I agreed to go. We drove from Burlington and stopped for a hike. Along the hike we came upon a waterfall and a pond. When we got to the pond he mentioned that he wanted to take his clothing off and go for a swim. He suggested that I do the same. I told him it was too cold and I opted to sit on the grass by the water while he continued to remove his clothing and went for a swim.

When he finished swimming and came out of the water, he walked toward me and then positioned himself with his genitalia in front of my face and said "You know what to do." I immediately said "no" and asked if we could leave. I remember feeling nervous because nobody else was there and I didn't know what was going to happen next. I tried to get up but he pushed me down and pinned me with my wrists so I couldn't move. I kept shouting to him that I wanted to go but he just wouldn't listen to me. At that point I was begging him to let me go and said I didn't want to have sex with him. It was at this point he forcibly removed my clothing and raped me.

I don't remember walking back from the pond to his car. I was in absolute shock that a fellow Coast Guard comrade would do this. I went to the barracks, took a shower, and hid from him. Later that night I received a text message on my cell phone from my rapist and shipmate. He stated that he had a letter for me and he placed it under my door. In the letter he stated how much he loved me and how sorry he was for what happened. I submitted the original letter to the Coast Guard legal team upon their request. The Coast Guard later denied having that letter of his rape confession.

I did not report the rape right away and I didn't get a rape kit done at the ER because of my earlier experiences. First I was beaten by my shipmate, and then the other incidents I was teased and blamed for. I figured I would be found at fault for this as well. I was scared of getting in trouble because I blamed myself for not being strong enough to stop the rape. I learned later that I was experiencing normal post-rape symptoms including denial, self-blame, and fear. I made the mistake of trying to put the entire incident out of my head.

I wanted to tell the executive petty officer. I was scared but I knew it had to be done. When I finally I started telling the XPO and within three sentences of what I said about my shipmate he told me "drop it." Once he heard that I wanted to press charges against my rapist he told me to leave his office.

A friend of mine heard about the rape and went to officers in Boston and gave them a general summary of what was going on. The Equal Employment Opportunity (EEO) officer called me and though I talked to him I didn't have the courage to tell him everything. The XPO in Burlington somehow found out and called me into the chief's office. The chief, XPO, and another first class petty officer stated that what I was doing was against Coast Guard policy and that I could get discharged if I talked to a petty officer who was not in my chain of command. They also found out that I spoken to the Equal Employment officer and suggested that I call him back and tell him that I would not press charges against the chief or the XPO.

They spent almost two hours trying to convince me that I should not be telling the EEO officer about what's going on at the station because "they could lose their job." They explained to me that the Coast Guard means more to them than their own family. They told me that they had wives and kids to support and tried to make me feel guilty for mentioning anything. The first class petty officer told me that this would end up going in front of the captain and that he would laugh when he heard a "non-rate trying to go against her chief." He said that I was just making a fool of myself and in court he would side with the chief and the XPO because I am just a non-rate.

They asked me if I had anything planned because I would be at the station for a long time. I informed them about an appointment scheduled with my civilian therapist through the Coast Guard's Employee Assistance Program and they said that I couldn't go. I also was not allowed to go "upstairs to the barracks or change out of uniform." I had to stay on the second deck and work until I told them that I would not be telling anyone about what happened at Station Burlington. I ended up having to clean off mud, shine all the metal in the mess deck, and other such jobs till late in the afternoon. Feeling defeated, I told the chief that I would not be telling anyone in Boston about my Burlington experience. I felt dismayed and realized that I would have to work under this command for the next few years. With that said, I thought it was best to not burn any bridges with them and just drop the issue even though I know what they were doing was wrong.

After this happened, I was in the process of getting boat-crew qualified and had all my requirements done except for a few that needed to be done while underway. The entire station was told to not allow me to go underway for no other reason but to punish me. I was forbidden to advance within the Coast Guard. Shortly after these incidents, my performance changed and command noticed and I was sent to South Portland, Maine to have a performance review done. While in Portland I worked really effectively because I was away from my rapist/shipmate, and when my fourteen days were up I received a good report and got all good reviews in Portland.

The chief in Portland called me into his office and said that I did a great job and that they would escort me back to Burlington and I started crying. I told him I couldn't go back to Burlington. He figured out something was wrong because just mentioning the word Burlington alone made me cry. He eventually said he wouldn't send me back but would send me to Boston because there would be a lot of people there that could help.

In Boston I was denied testing for any sexually transmitted diseases and for potential injuries that may have occurred during the rape.

My first weekend in Boston I was put on "restricted duty" and forbidden to leave the base. Even though I was showing obvious signs of Post-Traumatic Stress Disorder and Military Sexual Trauma, I did not receive any treatment. The lieutenant who was put in charge of finding me medical care stated that due to TRICARE policies it was difficult to find a doctor that deals with sexual assault survivors in the city of Boston. It took four months after the rape for me to see my first psychologist about my trauma.

I was assigned to work at "Coastie Joe's," the on-base coffee shop. My duties included cashier and making coffee. I eventually was told I could no longer work there by a commander because I was a "slut and flirted with the customers." When asked what he meant by flirting he said that I was "smiling and being polite."

In August 2006 I was admitted to the VA hospital in Brockton for inpatient psychological treatment. I was sent there because a lieutenant found me crying and thought I was suicidal. I was put on suicide watch while at the hospital and after a few days there the doctors said that I was dealing with PTSD and that my crying was the result of being raped and not a sign of being suicidal. They gave me Zoloft for depression but after a while I started feeling worse and felt the medication was to blame. The doctor at the VA agreed and we mutually decided that I'd get off the medication. I was sent back to Boston on August 8, 2006.

The next day I was transferred to the Force Optimization and Training branch in Boston. I was given a desk job and told that rape victims could not do any "real Coast Guard work." I was told to sit there and not talk to anyone, so I did that for the next eight months. I was told that they were actually doing me a favor for putting me in FOT and not on the MAA force. The MAA force is where those who are waiting to get court-martialed are assigned. During this time there were two Coast Guardsmen assigned on MAA duty and were awaiting court-martial for child pornography charges. Why was a rape survivor being put in the same category as two pedophiles?

On August 23, 2006, I was sent back to the Coast Guard Academy for a follow-up due to my being an inpatient at the VA. The psychologist's first reaction when seeing me there was anger. He was angry that I was an inpatient at the hospital especially since I was not suicidal. His main concern were the high costs of inpatient care. I went to the hospital against my will. I was sent there in tears, because of tears. How could this have been my fault? He was also angry that I had stopped taking Zoloft, and said that I was "refusing treatment" and forced me to start taking Zoloft again. I brought up the rape and he said that the rape wasn't why he's seeing me. He also said that I should "get over the rape" since I was no longer at Station Burlington. He then told me that I'll be recommended for a medical board for adjustment disorder and was escorted out.

During another visit with the psychologist he noted I was sexually active prior to the assault and knew my perpetrator. He argued that because this was true—and because they give out condoms and birth control in boot camp—that I was "fully prepared." I met with Coast Guard Investigative Service who investigated the alleged sexual assault. I met with them twice and had countless failed attempts to contact them to know the outcome of the investigation.

A lieutenant commander from District 1 legal team was assigned to be my legal advocate. According to him, it is dishonorable to "report a rape."

According to the Coast Guard's core values of honor, respect, and devotion to duty, how am I honoring and respecting my shipmate for bringing a rape allegation against him? He also said he didn't believe that I was assaulted, given that "One undergoes a security, background check to be able to serve in the Coast Guard. Only those that passed the criminal background check are able to serve and if he did not have a history of raping women in the past why would he be doing it now?" He also mentioned that I would go to prison unless I dropped the charges. Initially I refused to drop charges because I knew what happened to me, there was a confession by the rapist, and the evidence was there. I was naive in thinking that someone would actually do their job, put a criminal behind bars, but the system failed me. Eventually the threats from my lawyer were so severe and traumatizing that I had no other choice but to drop the charges.

The sexual assault allegation was not kept confidential. Almost everyone on base knew why I was transferred to Boston. On base I often heard my shipmates call me a "whore," "slut," and "a liar." Another E-3 told me that "You're hot, I'd love to rape you too." Unfortunately I do not know his name. I was also receiving death threats. One day, while living in the barracks at ISC Boston, at around two or three in the morning there was a knock on the door. When I answered it, there were two intoxicated men in civilian clothes that threatened me and tried to get into my barrack room. It got so bad that I had to move off base.

On May 24, 2007, I received an honorable discharge under narrative reasons of "unacceptable conduct." As a result of serving less than twenty-four months in the Coast Guard I am denied the GI Bill and a bonus that was promised to me by my recruiter. I am currently receiving ongoing medical treatment for Post-Traumatic Stress Disorder and Military Sexual Trauma at the Boston VA. The Boston VA confirmed that the psychologist of the United States Coast Guard misdiagnosed me with having adjustment disorder and personality disorder.

NATHAN PELD

Petty Officer, Second Class, United States
Navy, Nuclear Electronics Technician

Deployments: *USS Ronald Reagan*

Hometown: Green Bay, Wisconsin

Age at Winter Soldier: 27 years old

I served in the United States Navy from 1998 to 2004. I was a nuclear electronics technician aboard the *USS Ronald Reagan*. This placed me in an unusual situation because it was a pre-commissioning unit, which meant that I was there from the earliest stages of construction. So this also meant that most of the ship worked regular, 7 a.m. to 3 p.m., and we were able to go home at night; it was really great for us.

As a member of the Reactor Department, we were divided into four groups that worked rotating shift work, and this provided twenty-four hours of security and testing, and we worked jointly with the shipyard in these matters.

On one of these off-ships when there was a minimal crew on board, there was a young woman who was working in her divisional office. She had a direct superior come in and after speaking he dropped his pants and exposed himself to her. Fortunately, she recognized that this was not an off-color joke or the usual barrage of playful flirting but more of a flagrant violation. She took the proper method and reported this up her chain of command, and when this reached the senior enlisted commander in my department he took it and tried to initiate a cover-up. There were many reasons for this: because he hadn't actually hurt her, perhaps they could agree on a compromise, and because maybe from his perspective he didn't consider it a hostile environment. He was also two years away from retirement and her speaking out could have ruined his career at such a key moment for him.

She did not agree to this and went above her chain of command. When this account finally reached the upper chains of command and the two men had to explain themselves, the man who exposed himself was finally put into procedure for court-martial, and he was dishonorably discharged.

The darker side of this story was that the man who initiated the cover-up was given only a reprimand. He was trying to do what was "best for the department" and that was to keep us quiet and so only receiving a reprimand was the only action that was taken against him. This scene shows how members of the navy who try to play games of male dominance receive all but a free pass.

JEFF KEY

Lance Corporal, United States Marine Corps
Reserve, Light Armored Vehicle Technician ,
4th Light Armored Reconnaissance

Deployments: April 2003–June 2003,
from Kuwait to al-Hilla

Hometown: Salt Lake City, Utah

Age at Winter Soldier: 42 years old

I was thirty-four years old when I walked in that recruiting station. I did so for the same reasons that I'm sitting here today; I love America. I know these are dark times, but I have great hope for the future.

I'm an out queer man. I knew under Clinton's "Don't Ask, Don't Tell" policy that things would not be easy, but I wanted to serve bad enough that I went along with that policy. I was naive. Once you're in a fighting hole with someone who's sharing the deep contents of their soul and willing to take a bullet for you, and you for them, to manufacture some bogus life is ridiculous. I would not spit in their face by doing so.

I have to say that my experience of serving as a queer man in the military was very different than some. People are still assaulted and sometimes murdered for being gay in our military, and those who institutionalize government-mandated discrimination of any sort such as a ban on gays in the military is wrong. It's un-American. But those who think that lifting the ban on gays in the military will end homophobia are as naive as those who thought that in 1948 when we desegregated our troops that it ended racism. It did not.

I want to express gratitude for those marines who stood by me. They stood by me in war, they knew who I was, they knew everything about me, they stood by me in my wedding. They have gone very public and put themselves at risk to speak out on behalf of queers serving.

When I came back, I knew that I could not be a party to this occupation. I could not be true to my oath as a marine and continue to serve, so I went on CNN and came out of the closet to five million people and made them throw me out.

I heard too many stories about people who were coming out and getting deployed anyway. And I knew that because of my oath, my belief in God, and what I believe is right to do, I cannot participate in this very dangerous occupation.

At the core of this war machine is an ideology that is based on the gender paradigm and homophobia. That's why even in the twenty-first century just about the worst thing you can say to a straight teenage boy is that he's queer. I can tell you from personal experience that young straight men, otherwise good men, will go to great lengths and do horrible things to prove that they're not gay.

This is the only way I can explain the cruel way some of my fellow marines treated the kids who came up next to our vehicles during our deployment. It's the only way I can explain that some of my fellow marines thought it was fun to feed a stray dog antifreeze, which the dog found delicious, but causes a slow and painful death. I remember one night in Iraq some marines were trying to chase a mouse from underneath my tent. They were trying to kill it. They seemed thirsty for blood, any blood would do. It made me nervous. One lance corporal swung an ax handle at the mouse like a bat, before bringing down the blade and snuffing the life out of the innocent beast.

Somehow this idea of men are beings devoid of feelings and compassion and that women are weak and just a ball of emotions is at the center of all this. I can tell you now that my highest idea of someone who serves in our military has everything to do with dispelling these old ways of thinking around gender and sexuality, and everything to do with standing up for what our country supposedly stands for.

MARGARET STEVENS

Specialist, New Jersey Army National Guard, Medic

Deployments: New York City after 9/11

Hometown: Newark, New Jersey

Age at Winter Soldier: 28 years old

Gender and sexuality issues go to the core of the war itself, and I think that that's the point of the title of this panel.

I was at a club in Virginia last year, it was an 18-and-older club, so that meant that most of the girls were eighteen and the guys were like thirty. I see this guy and he's attractive and he has on a military shirt, he's a recruiter. You've got these big strong guys in this club trying to recruit these young, eighteen-year-old girls into the military. It's very clear that the process of sexual trauma begins at the point of recruitment, not at the point of basic training. For many of these young women, their first sexual encounter with a man is the recruiter, if they don't have a father figure, if they don't have brothers in their lives. That wasn't my experience. I didn't join in that sort of desperate state, but that's a reality for many people and I want you to keep that in mind.

In basic training there was a young, female recruit who was engaging in sexual relations with one of the drill sergeants. When we found that out, it was disgusting and demoralizing. It got exposed and he never tried to approach me or the other women and hit on us, but the dynamics were there.

I joined the New Jersey National Guard in 1997. I was a medic, a very woman-heavy field. We didn't have the same sort of experiences as women in mechanic fields do. When 9/11 happened our unit was called up to do post–9/11 relief. At that moment, I just figured my life would change. We were going to war. But what I also knew that I could get pregnant. So I said to myself, "What happens if I get pregnant?" Maybe I wouldn't have to go if I was having a baby. We'd have to be deployed in the next nine months and we could deploy a year later, I'd still have to go anyway. Then I'd have a three-month-old baby that I can't stay with because I waited too long or because I did it too quickly. This is the type of math that people do.

A lot of men think oh, you're a sellout or you're a punk. You joined the military, why are you gonna get pregnant? You see? This is the type of tension that happens. I don't think it's important to go into my experience, but I just want you to know that many women do get pregnant. Many women do end up having abortions and many women did have babies. After 9/11.

Who are these women? These members of the National Guard are mothers and grandmothers. So now you have guys at home saying "Baby, I'll go. You stay. Let me go for you," and we know that that's not reality. That's not how it works. When you get called up, you are the one that has to go.

I can speak on behalf of a good friend of mine who was raped and there was no evidence. That's a huge problem, that there's no evidence. When there's no evidence you don't qualify for benefits and you can't claim that you have PTSD because there's no documentation of the crime. When one does try to document the crime, they're coerced and told that they're a sellout, and other men who might want to be on your side are also coerced and made to feel like if they speak up they're turning against their own. That's not just against the women, because these young men have to live with that too. They have to decide whether they want to be on the side of the victim or the victimizer, when in fact we are all in a situation where all are being forced into an occupation that none of us are really happy about.

When we have women in command, will that solve the problem? There are people who are lobbying to say that women should be higher up and they should have more power. I'm not convinced that having women in command will change the nature of our situation in the occupation itself. There are women who are trying to fight, there are women who are trying to speak out. The military is scared out of its mind to have this panel right here. This panel is history. Because women are in combat now, and they're so scared that this is gonna get out.

THE CRISIS IN VETERANS' HEALTH CARE AND THE COSTS OF WAR AT HOME

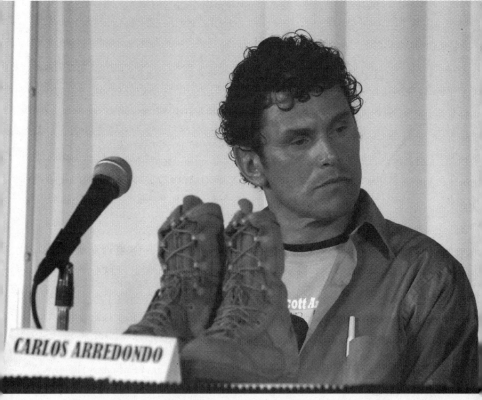

CARLOS ARREDONDO

Carlos Arredondo's son Alexander was killed in Iraq August 25, 2004.   PHOTO: MIKE HASTIE

INTRODUCTION

Eighteen American war veterans kill themselves every day.[1] One thousand former soldiers receiving care from the Department of Veterans Affairs attempt suicide every month.[2] More veterans are committing suicide than are dying in combat overseas. These are statistics that most Americans don't know, because the government has refused to tell them. Since the start of the Iraq War, official Washington has tried to present it as a war without casualties.

In fact, these statistics never would have come to light were it not for a class action lawsuit brought by Veterans for Common Sense and Veterans United for Truth on behalf of the 1.7 million Americans who have served in Iraq and Afghanistan. The two groups allege the Department of Veterans Affairs has systematically denied mental-health care and disability benefits to veterans returning from the conflict zones. The case, officially known as *Veterans for Common Sense v. Peake*, went to trial in April 2008 at a federal courthouse in San Francisco. The two sides will no doubt be battling it out in court for years, but the case is already having an impact.

That's because over the course of the two-week trial, the VA was compelled to produce a series of documents that show the extent of the crisis affecting wounded soldiers.

"Shh!" began one e-mail from Dr. Ira Katz, the head of the VA's Mental Health Division, advising a media spokesperson not to tell *CBS News* that one thousand veterans receiving care at the VA try to kill themselves every month. "Our suicide prevention coordinators are identifying about 1,000 suicide attempts per month among the veterans we see in our medical facilities. Is this something we should (carefully) address ourselves in some sort of release before someone stumbles on it?" the e-mail concludes.[3]

Leading Democrats on the Senate Veterans Affairs Committee immediately called for Katz's resignation. The chair of the House Committee on Veterans Affairs, Bob Filner (D-CA), weighed in as well. "We should all be angry about what has gone on here," Filner said. "This is a matter of life and death for the veterans that we are responsible for and I think there was criminal negligence in the way this was handled. If we do not admit, assume or know then the problem will continue and people will die. If that's not criminal negligence, I don't know what is."[4]

It's also part of a pattern. The high number of veteran suicides weren't the only government statistics the Bush administration was forced to reveal because of the class-action lawsuit. Another set of documents presented in court showed that in the six months leading up to March 31, 2008, a total of 1,467 veterans died waiting to learn if their disability claim would be approved by the government. A third set of documents showed that veterans who appeal a VA decision to deny their disability claim have to wait an average of 1,608 days, or nearly four and a half years, for their answer.[5]

Other casualty statistics are not directly concealed, but are also not made public on a regular basis. For example, the Pentagon reports regularly on the numbers of American troops "wounded" in Iraq (32,224 as of June 1, 2008) but neglects to mention that it has two other categories: "injured" and "ill" (together 39,430).[6] All three of these categories represent soldiers who are so damaged physically they have to be medically evacuated to Germany for treatment, but splitting up the numbers minimizes the sense of casualties in the public consciousness.

Here's another number that we don't often hear discussed in the media: 287,790.[7] That's the number of returning Iraq and Afghanistan war veterans who had filed a disability claim with the Department of Veterans Affairs as of March 25, 2008. That figure was not announced to the public at a news conference, but had to be obtained using the Freedom of Information Act.

Each number in these statistics represents the suffering of a patriotic American who signed up for the U.S. Armed Forces and agreed to go anywhere in the world at the order of their commander in chief. As the testimony offered at Winter Soldier shows, veterans have been lied to twice—first about the reasons for going to war and second about the government's commitment to take care of them when they get home.

ZOLLIE PETER GOODMAN
Petty Officer, United States Navy,
Flight Director, Salvage Crew Operator
Deployments: *USS John F. Kennedy;*
November 2004, Fallujah
Hometown: Gainesville, Florida
Age at Winter Soldier: 24 years old

Regardless of your political viewpoints, regardless of your personal feelings, one day the United States military will leave Iraq. When we do, all we will have to show for it is thousands of dead Americans. In the meantime, the war ends every single day for our soldiers, because someone is discharged from the United States military every single day. They're discharged with no assistance getting into the VA system. Some people are discharged without knowing that they qualify for veterans' benefits, like I was.

I served on the *USS John F. Kennedy* and deployed to the Persian Gulf in 2004. I worked as an aircraft director on the flight deck. I was one of those guys with the yellow vest and the orange sticks that helps direct the planes on take-off and landing. But in the fall of 2004, I was pulled off my ship and was sent to take part in the second siege of Fallujah, which we called Operation Phantom Fury.

Fallujah was declared a "free-fire zone" in November 2004 and we told the civilian population that they had to leave because the entire city was going to be deemed hostile territory. Some of them left. They carried TVs or food and sat outside the city and waited for the firefight to be over so they could go home. Some of them didn't leave. At the time, that possibility didn't even enter my head, that some of these people wouldn't leave.

We are all trained to kill, and we do it well. The standard procedure that we followed in Fallujah whether written or unwritten was to leave dead Iraqis in the streets to be buried by their own. This presented a problem because the sewage system was shut down so sewage started to back up into the streets. There were dead bodies floating in sewage. The smell, I'll never forget the smell. I can smell it right now.

We would just leave the dead Iraqis in the streets and they piled up. It was disgusting. We ended up sighting in our weapons on these dead bodies. We'd been trained to keep our weapons "on point." You always want your weapon to be sighted in. So when we didn't have a target to shoot we sighted our weapons on dead people and dead animals. That happened a lot at the tail end of Operation Phantom Fury.

Later on I was discharged with no assistance getting into the VA system. The processing of my application for VA health care took at least three months. When I was finally able to request mental health over the phone, I was told that I could not get an appointment for three more months, and I did not make an appointment. A few days later I looked up the law, and the law says that the VA only has a thirty-day maximum to provide an appointment for someone requesting an appointment. So I called this wonderful organization back and I cited the laws of our wonderful country, and I was given an appointment, and like every other appointment that I've ever had from the Veterans Administration it was thirty days later.

So I went and I showed up at this appointment, and I was inducted into what is a processing system set up to deter people from seeking help. I was spoken to with no compassion. Every single phone call I make to the VA I'm asked if I'm going to kill myself or somebody else in the most inhumane way you could imagine, by the most inhumane people you could imagine.

So after going through this process, the first thing they tried to do was medicate me. No therapy was recommended. Medications were recommended. They gave me three different medications. The first was Trazodone. The second was Paxil. And the third was gabapentin, a generic form of Neurontin. My doctor did not give me any information on these medications. He told me that PTSD treatment is not a science and that there is no science to it, and that you can mix and match these medications, and something may work for you that doesn't work for another vet.

So I left my appointment that day, and I went home and I did research on the medications that I was given. And I found out that the main side effect of all three medications is suicidal thoughts and suicidal tendencies. And that's disgusting, and that man should be disgusted with himself, and every doctor that does that should be disgusted with himself.

So upon deciding not to take the medication, I decided I would try therapy. Once again I called the VA and requested therapy. I was told that I couldn't get an appointment for several months, and I cited the law again, and I was given an appointment thirty days later. So now I get to go to a fifteen-minute therapy session once every thirty days. And when I show up to my fifteen-minute therapy session, there's fifteen other Vietnam vets that have the same 8 a.m. appointment that I do, and we all wait around in the lobby.

Every single one of these vets is there seeking help and treatment for the same thing that I'm seeking help and treatment for, and they're all thirty years older than I am. They've been in the system thirty years longer. They've been taking the same medications for thirty years, the same therapists for thirty years, and they're still there and they still have the same problem. So obviously it doesn't work. There's no solution with the current situation.

When I'm not at the VA and I'm around town, everywhere I go I see homeless vets, because one-third of the homeless population is veterans, and that's disgusting. It is so detrimental. It is so frustrating. It is so angering to me and I'm sure to every single vet in this room that has ever walked into a VA hospital on their own accord to seek treatment or to somehow comfort the people that are trapped inside of these establishments.

My name is Zollie Peter Goodman. I'm a proud warrior and a prouder patriot, and that's my problem with the VA.

ERIC ESTENZO

Corporal, United States Marine Corps Reserve, MOS

Deployments: March 2003–September 2003, from Kuwait to al-Hilla

Hometown: Los Angeles, California

Age at Winter Soldier: 32 years old

Within the final three weeks of our tour, I had a non-combat back injury. The battalion aid station officers told me that if I was injured in country, I would have to stay in Iraq or go to Germany for medical care. They said it would be in my best interest to not say anything until we get back to Camp Pendleton. So I waited, injured, without even my command knowing that I was injured.

When I got back to Camp Pendleton, I immediately sought care with the Navy Medical Center, and their response was outstanding. The day after I reported my back injury I was actually seen. I was getting therapy, and I thought that this was great. "I served my country. I did my tour in Iraq, and I'm being taken care of." That is exactly what I expected. I expected a two-way system, where I serve and then they support. I thought that everything was working out for me.

When I was honorably discharged in 2005, I looked forward to a new chapter in my life. I was in garrison at Camp Pendleton. They told me what was going to happen. They told me that my medical records would be transferred and the VA health-care system will take care of me. There was all of this good information that led me to believe I would be taken care of. I really trusted the system.

When I got out of the military, I became a full-time student. At that time, I enrolled in the Long Beach VA Healthcare System. Today, three years after returning from Iraq, I haven't even gotten past the paperwork. I've gotten X-rays and MRIs, but that's where it ended.

I don't understand why there is such a delay. What's the issue? It doesn't make sense. I just got paperwork and talk about how I should conduct myself now that I'm a civilian, and that's where it ended.

From 2005 until 2006 they sent me letters while I waited on my disability claim. I had adjustment issues. I needed to see a psychiatrist. I needed to get some kind of counseling to figure out what was going on with me, because at the time I didn't think PTSD was an issue. They informed me that I had two years' worth of free medical care, but with appointments one or two months apart, two years' worth of free medical service is nothing. And because I was a full-time student, it was even harder because they wouldn't schedule appointments around my schoolwork.

I began to realize that adjusting to civilian life was going be challenging. I tried to be optimistic about my future, but even after I got my AA degree I was still dealing with the VA health care system, which was more of a roadblock than anything else.

After graduation, I couldn't find a job. The jobs I did find wouldn't pay enough. I left the military with $17,000 in the bank and good credit. But the $17,000 I saved went to zero. My expenses were overwhelming and I couldn't pay them. I was having adjustment issues with jobs. My credit score went very low. I couldn't believe it. This must have been how Vietnam veterans felt when they came back home.

I heard about Iraq Veterans Against the War through a friend of mine, Jeff Key, who served with me in the 4th Light Armored Reconnaissance. We touched base when I didn't think I was going to be able to help myself. He told me if I went over to his place in Hollywood I'd be able to stay there, but it wasn't immediate. Jeff was traveling and no one was there. So this was considered couch-surfing. I didn't consider myself homeless.

So I ended up sleeping in my car for one day. I was in Hollywood. I decided to walk around, see if I could find a job. I reached this corner, I can't remember the name of the block, but there was a food wagon that was serving free food to homeless people. I decided to take that opportunity to eat some free food. At first I was thinking, "I'm just hungry and this is free food, and I'm gonna go for it."

I stood in line and noticed the Friends Helping Friends organization was there with a video camera documenting homelessness. As I stood there watching everybody else around me, I looked at myself and I thought, "I'm now an Iraq War vet. I'm standing in a line with homeless people, being served free food and this is actually happening to me."

At that moment reality hit, and it hit so hard that suicidal thoughts began. I broke down several times. I cracked the day after that. Once I was able to get back to Jeff's place, I told him many times about ending my life because this is not exactly how I wanted it to be. I lost dignity, self-respect. I was in a very dark place for a considerable amount of time.

I had a relationship with a girl. That went away as well. She couldn't understand the situation I was in, so I ended that relationship. The school situation never picked up, and I ended up having to find a job that barely paid anything. It was through Jeff Key that I found my way back into life. He introduced me to Iraq Veterans Against the War, and through them I found a place that helps vets recuperate and continue their lives after the military.

As I pulled my life back together, I was again surprised that the VA system wouldn't help me, even at this time of need. I was reluctant to go back to them, but I was told if I didn't go back then they'd never know, and I'd be another casualty of the system. So I did go back and, unfortunately, I'm back at square one. They still want me to fill out more paperwork. That's where I stand to this day.

ELI WRIGHT

Sergeant, United States Army, Medic

Deployment:
   September 2003–September 2004, Ramadi

Hometown: Denver, Colorado

Age at Winter Soldier: 26 years old

This is my own experience. These are my beliefs and my opinions. I'm not speaking on behalf of the military or the chain of command. I'm not representing anybody's opinions or beliefs but my own.

I'm currently awaiting a medical discharge from the army for injuries sustained in Iraq and after I came home. I don't have any glorious war story, no Purple Heart for my injuries, and I think that's the reason it's been so difficult for me to get treatment. I was in a vehicle accident in Iraq. It wasn't anything hostile. It was just a driver not paying attention. I wasn't wearing a seat belt. We didn't have functional seat belts. We didn't have a functional lock on the door either.

So when we were hit I was ejected from the vehicle. I sustained a back and a neck injury. I hit my head pretty hard. Fortunately, I was wearing a helmet. My adrenalin level was pumping, so I wasn't in a whole lot of pain at the time, and I was able to just continue mission. "Charlie Mike," as they say.

So I kept at it, but I started having problems, chronic back and neck pain. After coming home from Iraq I sustained another injury. It was just a football injury during unit physical training, nothing spectacular there. I had dislocated my shoulder and had torn cartilage in it, but I was only given a quick X-ray and some Motrin. Those of you in the military know how much they like to give out Motrin.

I started working in the neuroscience ward at Walter Reed, treating a lot of patients with traumatic brain injuries. I'd been back from Iraq for almost a year, but I was still trying to get treatment for my back and neck injuries. I had recurrent dislocations throughout that time. I started having memory loss, headaches, and dizziness. That's when I started recognizing that I was having a lot of the symptoms of mild TBI, but I couldn't get a screening for it. There really was no screening process for it then and in large part there still isn't.

Fast forward. Over the last year, I've been stationed at Fort Drum. When I got there I was given orders to deploy. By that time I'd become fed up with not being able to get treatment for my injuries. I wasn't capable of doing my job. One of my biggest concerns was that if I couldn't do my job, other people might die.

I addressed those concerns to the medical screening team. Over two years after the injury, they finally looked at my shoulder injury and agreed I wasn't fit for deployment. I gave them my MRI results and they said, "You should have had surgery a long time ago."

They did the operation, and then I went through six months of physical therapy. After that, they told me I had plateaued. I'd gotten all of the good out of the physical therapy that I was going to get, but my shoulder is in worse shape than it was prior to the surgery. Because they waited so long, my shoulder is disabled for the rest of my life.

I was supposed to be medically discharged but nothing happened for almost six months. I was waiting for appointments for both psychiatric and physical issues. I asked questions but didn't get answers.

I know my problems aren't the only ones. My problems are minor compared to the stories of other soldiers for whom I've provided peer counseling. This is a systemic issue, and it's not any one doctor's or any one commander's fault.

The only recourse that I was able to find was speaking to the media. Two days after I spoke with the media I saw a traumatic brain injury specialist. A physical therapist rescreened my shoulder, diagnosing more problems. After six months with almost no progress, I got proper care two days after my story was published in the New York Times.

We all know how many problems there are with VA health care, but *military* health care doesn't get much attention. Soldiers are afraid to speak out. It's time soldiers become proactive and demand proper health care.

We enlisted. We stepped up to serve our country and we haven't asked for a whole lot in return. Proper health care should be, at a bare minimum, what we're entitled to. The fact that we're not getting it makes me sick, because I have seen too many of my brothers and sisters suffering, and we are tired of suffering. We need to demand that we be taken care of.

ADRIENNE KINNE

Sergeant, United States Army Reserve, Voice Interpreter

Deployments: Classified

Hometown: Augusta, Georgia

Age at Winter Soldier: 31 years old

I served on active duty in the United States Army from 1994 to 1998 as an Arabic linguist and military intelligence. I then transferred to the United States Army Reserve, where I served from 1998 to 2004. I was activated and stationed stateside right after 9/11 for about two years. I went through this system twice, once before 9/11 and the current wars and once after, and I personally witnessed a complete transformation in the way the process was handled. In 1998 I received a complete and thorough end-of-service physical. As part of the out-processing system, a VA representative sat with me and reviewed every single page of my medical file and filled out a VA disability claim for me.

In 2003, with thousands upon thousands of Reserve and National Guard servicemembers being deactivated through Fort Bragg, they told us if we wanted an end-of-service physical we would have to wait at Fort Bragg for six to eight weeks or longer, in these run-down World War II barracks out in the backwoods. The message was clear. Don't ask for an end-of-service physical. In addition, there was no VA representative helping people file a claim or reviewing our medical files. There was nobody telling us that we were eligible or how to get into the system. When a soldier is leaving the military, you have a window of opportunity to get into the VA system, but if you miss that opportunity it's so much harder to get in afterwards.

When I left the Reserves, I finished my education. I really wanted to continue serving veterans, so I decided to work at the VA. In 2004 and 2005 I did internships at the VA in Georgia. After I graduated I got a job at the VA in Richmond, Virginia where I worked as a research assistant on a study looking at Post-Traumatic Stress Disorder and traumatic brain injury, because the symptoms of these two illnesses are incredibly similar.

The research group wanted to develop a mechanism to screen returning soldiers for traumatic brain injury. There were a lot of incredibly educated, well-informed people establishing this traumatic brain injury screening. Before we could make it happen, I was on a conference call when somebody said, "Wait a second. We can't start this screening process. If we start screening for traumatic brain injury, tens of thousands of soldiers will screen positive. We do not have resources to take care of these people. We cannot do the screening."

Medical ethics say that if you know somebody has a problem you have to treat them, so they didn't want to know about the problem since they didn't have the resources to treat it. But I think it's incumbent upon all VA workers to find every area that we need addressed, and to demand that we get the resources to meet those needs.

Former VA secretary Jim Nicholson said that to meet the needs of returning veterans, they wanted to prioritize OIF and OEF veterans, which sounds great. Prioritizing always has a nice ring to it. But if you prioritize one group of veterans, another group has to do without. The VA needs to address the fact that we have hundreds of thousands of new veterans entering a system that has not grown to meet the demands of these two occupations. No veteran should have to go without.

The VA's mission to care for our nation's veterans is one of awesome responsibility. I personally believe that the best preventative health care for our soldiers is not to use them to fight illegal occupations. But so long as our government is going to force soldiers to continue fighting, I would call upon all workers at the VA to remember our pledge to serve and provide for our returning veterans.

It's also important to realize that we do not lose our free speech rights just because we're federal employees. We all know that behind the red tape there are just not enough resources to treat people. It is incumbent upon all VA employees to continue fighting, and fighting vocally, until we have all the resources necessary to take care of our veterans.

JOYCE AND KEVIN LUCEY, PARENTS OF JEFFREY LUCEY

Corporal, United States Marine Corps Reserve, MOS (convoy driver), 6th Motor Transportation Battalion

Deployments: February–July 2003, from Kuwait to Iraq

Hometown: Belchertown, Massachusetts

Date of Death: June 22, 2004 (23 years old)

Joyce Lucey

Jeffrey's death should never have happened. He was caught between the humanity of what he saw and what he had to do. My son was let down first by the government, who sent him to fight their war of choice and destroyed his soul, and then by the VA.

The tragedy is not that one marine has committed suicide, but that this continues to happen four years after our son's death, countless others' names that will never be placed on a memorial wall, though they are causalities of the emotional battlefield that rages on well after the guns and missiles have been silenced.

Jeffrey told me that he only wanted to help people. His voice is now silenced, but ours is not, and we intend to follow Jeff's wishes by adding our voices to others, demanding that our government be held accountable for its actions or lack thereof.

Jeffrey Lucey, the young man who in January 2003 was sent to Kuwait to participate in an invasion that he did not support was not the same young man who stepped off the bus in July. Our marine physically returned to us, but his spirit died somewhere in Iraq. As we celebrated his homecoming, Jeff masked his anger,

Corporal Jeffrey Lucey hung himself in his parents' basement on June 22, 2004, after the Department of Veterans Affairs refused to treat him.

Jeff was a convoy driver and participated in the invasion of Iraq. On March 20, he entered in his journal, "At 10:30 p.m. a scud landed in our vicinity. We were just falling asleep when a shock wave rattled through our tent. The noise was just short of blowing out your eardrums. Everyone's heart truly skipped a beat, and the reality of where we are and what's happening hit home." His last entry is, "We now just had a gas alert and it's past midnight. We will not sleep. Nerves are on edge." The invasion had begun and Jeff never had time to put in another entry.

The letters we received from him were brief and sanitized, but in April 2003 he wrote to his girlfriend of six years, "There are things I wouldn't want to tell you or my parents, because I don't want you to be worried. Even if I did tell you, you'd probably think I was just exaggerating. I never want to fight in a war again. I've seen and done enough horrible things to last me a lifetime." This is the baggage that my son carried when he stepped off that bus that sunny July day at Fort Nathan Hale, New Haven, Connecticut.

Over the next several months we missed the signs that Jeffrey was in trouble. In July he went to Cape Cod with his girlfriend, and she found him distant. He didn't want to walk on the beach. He later told a friend at college that he had seen enough sand to last a lifetime.

At his sister's wedding the following month, he told his grandmother that "you could be in a room full of people, but still feel so alone." That fall we learned that Jeff had been vomiting nearly every day since his return. That continued until the day he died.

On Christmas Eve his sister found him at home, drinking. He was standing by the refrigerator. He grabbed his dog tags, and he tossed them to her and called himself a murderer. Later we learned that the dog tags belonged to two Iraqi soldiers that he felt or he knew he was personally responsible for their death. He was wearing these to honor the men, not as a trophy, he told the therapist he saw for the last seven weeks of his life. In February he told me he dreamed that these men were coming after him in an alleyway.

Throughout the spring and summer of 2004, our family watched Jeff fall apart. He was depressed and drinking. Attending community college was very difficult. He had panic attacks, feeling that the other students were staring at him. He started taking Klonopin and Prozac. He had trouble sleeping, nightmares, poor appetite, and he was isolating himself in his room. He couldn't focus on school and was unable to take his final exams. Although he had previously been an excellent athlete, now his balance was badly compromised by Klonopin and alcohol.

He confided in his younger sister that he had picked out a rope and a tree near the brook behind our home, but told her, "Don't worry. I'd never do that. I wouldn't hurt Mom and Dad."

He was adamant that we not tell the marines of his condition, fearing a psychological discharge and the stigma associated with PTSD. He was reluctant to go to the VA for the same reason.

His dad called and explained what was happening with our son, and they said it was classic PTSD. He should come in as soon as possible. They assured Jeff that they would not discuss his condition with his marine command. The problem was getting Jeffrey to go in. Every day it was, "Tomorrow. I'll go in tomorrow. I'm tired."

The day he went in he blew a 0.328 blood alcohol content, and VA administrators involuntarily committed him for four days. It took six employees to take Jeffrey down. He had gotten out the door and ran out into the parking area.

During his four-day stay, he felt like he was being warehoused. He saw the admitting psychiatrist and did not have another appointment until his discharge. He told the VA about the three methods of suicide he had contemplated—overdose, suffocation, or hanging. When he was admitted, he even told them he had a hose to choke himself. None of this was relayed to us. Instead, on Tuesday, June 1, 2004, he was released.

The VA told us that he would not be assessed for PTSD until he was alcohol free. But as with so many veterans, Jeff was self-medicating. He often told us that alcohol was the only way he could sleep at night. The VA said that we might consider kicking him out of the house so he would hit rock-bottom and then realize he needed help.

Jeff said he had wanted to tell the psychiatrist conducting his discharge interview about the bumps in the Iraqi road that were the children his marine convoy was told not to stop for and just not look back. He decided not to reveal this deeply sensitive information when the psychiatrist interrupted their session three times to answer phone calls.

On June 3, on a Dunkin' Donuts run, two days after he was released from the hospital, he totaled our car. Was it a suicide attempt? We're never going to know. No drinking was involved. I was terrified I was losing my little boy. I asked him where he was. He touched his chest and he said, "Right here, Mom." On the 5th he arrived at Holyoke Community College

to watch the graduation of his sister. This was supposed to be his graduation also, but he wasn't able to take his finals. How he drove his car there
we'll never know. He was so impaired.

We managed to get him home, but his behavior got worse. He was very depressed. His sisters and brother-in-law and my dad took him back to the VA.

When they arrived at the VA, he refused to go inside the building. VA
administrators decided that he was neither suicidal nor homicidal without
ever consulting anyone with the proper medical expertise. Our daughters
called home in a panic saying it didn't look like the VA was going to keep
their brother.

In their records the VA says Jeffrey's grandfather pleaded for someone
to help his grandson. My father lost his only brother in World War II. He
was twenty-two years old. He was now watching his only grandson self-de-
structing at twenty-three.

When we learned Jeff was coming back, Kevin and I went through each
room in our house. We took his knives, his bottles, anything we felt he
could use to harm himself. I took a step stool, a dog leash, anything I
thought could trigger something. We disabled his car, not only to protect
Jeff but to protect others from him.

Kevin called the civilian authorities. They said they couldn't do anything because he was drinking. My child was struggling to survive, and no
one would help us. The VA did not follow up with us even though he was in
crisis. We had no guidance about what to say to him or how to handle the
situation. We felt isolated, abandoned, and alone. While the rest of the
country lived on, going to Disneyworld, shopping, living their daily lives,
our days consisted of fear, apprehension, helplessness, watched this young
man, our son, being consumed by this cancer that ravaged his soul.

I sat on the deck of our home with a person who was impersonating my
son, and listened to him while he recounted bits and pieces of his time in
Iraq. Then he would grind his fist into his hand and say, "You could never
understand."

On Friday, June 11, a girl who'd grown up down the street called to say
that Jeff had climbed out his window and gotten into her car, looking for
beer. When Jeff came home, he was dressed in cammies with two Ka-Bars
knives, a modified pellet gun, and he was carrying a six-pack. He had just
wanted that beer. There was a sad smile on his face like a lost soul. When I

told him how concerned I was about him, he said, "Don't worry, Mom. No matter what I do I always come back."

Later, his girlfriend was talking to him on our deck, and she said tears were streaming down his face. The words to ".45," a song by the heavy-metal group Shine Down, that he listened to over and over again described him:

> In these times of doing what you're told
> You keep these feelings, no one knows
> What ever happened to the young man's heart
> Swallowed by pain, as he slowly fell apart
>
> And I'm staring down the barrel of a .45,
> Swimming through the ashes of another life
> No real reason to accept the way things have changed
> Staring down the barrel of a .45

After Jeffrey died on June 22, we found a note in the cellar. It said, "I am truly embarrassed of the man I became, and I hope you can try to remember me only as a child, when I was happy, proud, and enjoyed life."

Kevin Lucey

Jeffrey went through a lot during the intervening weeks. On June 22 the VA finally drafted a letter for Jeffrey, which was setting up an appointment for him on July 13. Regretfully, he wouldn't be able to make that appointment.

On the evening of Monday, June 21, I returned home and Jeffrey was in a total rage. I've never seen him like this. He was totally irate about the war, about his treatment at the VA, about so many different things. At about 7:30, I finally resorted to calling the Vet Center. The people at the Vet Center and the people at the VA are very, very good people. The angel who answered us at the Vet Center that evening calmed me down, and then got Jeffrey to calm down wonderfully.

Just before midnight, Jeffrey asked me for the second time in ten days if he could sit on my lap and if I could rock him for a while, and we did. We sat there for about forty-five minutes and I was rocking Jeff, and we were in total silence. As his private therapist said, it was his last harbor and his last place of refuge.

The next day I came home. It was about 7:15. I held Jeff one last time as I lowered his body from the rafters and took the hose from around his neck.

• • •

As a result of our family's experiences in May and June 2004, and our attempts to help him, we offer these few observations. First, why must the veteran meet the system's needs? Was not the VA health-care system developed to meet the needs of our veterans?

We were promised that steps would be taken in a timely manner to assure there would not be another Jeffrey. But two-and-a-half years after our Jeff died, there was Jonathan Schulze of Stewart, Minnesota. He died on January 16, 2007, in the identical fashion of our son, being turned away from the VA..

What was the purpose of the March 2007 *Washington Post* Walter Reed exposé and the government's immediate verbal reaction that they would address the issues? And then the *CBS News* investigation in November, reporting that the most up-to-date data indicated that an average of 120 veterans commit suicide each week? In the midst of all this, the Dole-Shalala Report was issued. People took note and we asked, "What has been done?" The Joshua Omvig bill has turned into law, but that is only the first item on a long list of necessary improvements for soldier and veteran health care.

Many say the words, "Honor and support our troops," but very few mean them. All people do is talk. Even as we talk today, how many more of our beloved troops and veterans have put nooses around their necks or loaded bullets in their chambers, their eyes filled with tears as they seek refuge from their agonies?

This is not moral. This is not ethical. We ask: Where is the rage? We call upon you to help us right this terrible wrong. Our family is suing the VA and this government for failing our son. Though there will never be a memorial to our loved ones, let their names never fade from your hearts or your memories: Walter Padilla, T.J. Sweet, Jason Cooper, Philip Kent, and so many more. Jeffrey is not the only tragedy. We are not the only family. We stand proudly with Military Families Speak Out and Gold Star Families for Peace and especially with all of you today.

CARLOS ARREDONDO, FATHER OF ALEXANDER ARREDONDO

Lance Corporal, United States Marine Corps,
Fire Team Leader

Deployments: January–September 2003;
May–August 2004, Nassariya, Najaf

Hometown: Randolph, Massachusetts

Killed in Action: August 25, 2004, awarded
Bronze Star with Combat V (20 years old)

This is my family. This is my dream.

I was born in Costa Rica. I came here as an illegal alien, and I did the best I could to take care of my family. It is the most beautiful thing that happened in my life. I call my sons my American dreams, and I thank God every minute for my experience with them, because they are my greatest teachers.

This is my son Alexander.

Alexander Arredondo at his high school graduation. Shortly before his graduation, Marine Corps recruiters visited Alex's high school and offered him a $20,000 bonus to join the military, money he never received.

PHOTO: CARLOS AND MELINDA ARREDONDO

That was the moment the recruiters went to his high school to seduce him with $20,000 cash to sign up—so many thousands of dollars for him to go into the military at the age of seventeen. They only required one parent to sign the consent form for a minor to join the military. The other parent is left behind. That's what happened to me.

I am not a sperm donor. This is my son, who I loved very much. They didn't have the respect to ask me if it was okay for him to go. They expect that they can grab our sons and daughters from anywhere they want, no matter if they're English or Spanish. They're seducing our sons with so many fake promises.

My son never had the opportunities they promised when he joined. He didn't get the cash and he didn't go to school. The signing bonus they promised is not even enough to go college, unless you're going to a community college. The liars! They didn't tell him. My son is one more victim of this immoral, illegal war. It is affecting the whole world.

Alexander wrote many, many letters home. In these letters, he speaks for himself. In one he wrote, "Tonight we were in a car chase and we picked up a guy with a grenade. I watched the whole damn thing. It didn't have to happen. I love you and miss you."

Alexander Arredondo on a convoy operation in Najaf, Iraq; July 30, 2004.
PHOTO: CARLOS AND MELINDA ARREDONDO

This is Alexander during his final days in the battle with Mutqtada al-Sadr in the old city of Najaf. My son is being carried in this truck like a guinea pig. He is anyone's target. This is outrageous, how they put our sons and daughters in this kind of situation.

One more letter from Alexander. "It looks like I am going to be stuck in Iraq forever. It sucks, it's hot, it smells, and I'm quite miserable." Alex's letters start changing from proud and honorable to miserable.

In another letter, Alexander explained the circumstances in which he was living. He was hoping to come home and go back to school. There was his girlfriend, Sheila. He was hoping to take care of his family.

Alexander was killed on August 25, 2004, in the old city of Najaf, where the marines' one-four battalion was cut off for four days in a four-story building. He was struck by a bullet in his left temple, which opened his head an inch and a half. Alexander was twenty years and twenty days old when he died. He spoke through his last few hours and told of the miserable life he was living there.

Many sons and daughters are coming back from war with broken bodies and broken minds. If my son were back home today, he probably would be in the VA system, in which case I'd be very concerned about our situation as well.

But my son took up his own path in life. He's resting in peace.

This is something that happens every few hours to families across the nation. Five years of war in Iraq, with more than four thousand casualties.

Alexander
Arredondo
lying in state
before burial.
PHOTO: CARLOS AND
MELINDA
ARREDONDO

I say thank God for this picture, because it teaches me a lot. It's been helping me a lot as well. This is the cost of the war at home. My son, Lance Corporal Alexander Arredondo, is lying in an open casket. And I thank God for the opportunity, because not many families in Iraq or the United States have the precious moment to say one last thing to your son with an open casket. I shared this moment with many other families and my heart goes to every single one.

This is the casualty at home. This is what happened when they came to notify me about the death of my son. That day also was my birthday. When I saw them coming, I thought my son was back because I saw their uniforms. I asked them to leave my house after they delivered the news.

I asked them to leave for more than a half-hour, and their pity was deep. They told me to go and nap for a half-hour. They left. I locked myself in their Marine Corps van, covered myself with gasoline, and set myself and the van on fire. I ended up more than 20 percent burned, with second- and third-degree burns. Because of what happened that day I spent one week in the hospital. They charged me $43,710.00. I didn't have the money. They put a lien on my house. A week later I buried my son in Boston. This was in Hollywood, Florida.

When members of the Marine Corps came to inform Carlos Arredondo of his son's death, he took a sledgehammer and smashed their van's windshield and climbed inside. Then Carlos locked himself inside the van, doused himself and the van with gasoline, and lit a propane torch. He suffered second- and third-degree burns over 20 percent of his body.

PHOTO: CARLOS AND MELINDA ARREDONDO

This is only one story of over four thousand families. They each go through the notification moments, when they come to tell you.

This is how I'm going around the country grieving my son. This is my pain. This is my loss. This is the First Amendment of the Constitution. They allow me to participate. As a father it's an obligation to honor my son and this country, to do anything I can to end this war. We can do it.

FERNANDO SUAREZ DEL SOLAR, FATHER OF JESUS ALBERTO SUAREZ DEL SOLAR

Lance Corporal, United States Marine Corps, MOS, 1st Light Armored Reconnaissance Battalion, 1st Marine Division

Hometown: Escondido, California

Killed in Action: March 27, 2003 (20 years old)

I visited Iraq in December 2003 with a family delegation. Global Exchange, Code Pink, Veterans for Peace, and the Alaro Organization gave me beautiful support for going to Iraq, because we needed to find the place my son died. I needed to show the Iraqi families that ordinary American people do not support the occupation, and that like Iraqi people who have lost a member of their family, American people have also lost members of their family in the war.

I had an opportunity to meet with families in Iraq who lost two, three, four, five members at the same time. These people opened their doors and their hearts and gave me a beautiful welcome.

When my son died, it made me crazy. I have a grandson. Jesus had a sixteen-month-old baby, only sixteen months old. When Jesus died, everybody cried in the house, and my grandbaby watched everybody and did not understand what happened. I guarded my grandson. I went to the park and played with him, because he is mine.

I didn't have an opportunity to cry for my son. I didn't have the opportunity because the government told me, "Your son died with a shot to the head. It's impossible for you to see the body because the face is destroyed and it's not good for the family. We will not pay for the funeral for you, because you chose your own cemetery."

Much later, I learned that the military lied to me. My son did not die when he received the shot to the head. Jesus died when he stepped on an illegal American cluster bomb and waited two hours for medical assistance. Then he died.

167

I miss my son. I cry every single day for Jesus. It's been five years. On March 27, it will be five years since my son died in Iraq. But when I come in here today with Iraq Veterans Against the War, and I see Camilo, and I see Juan, and I see Jethro, I see Jesus. This is my new family. These are my boys. My sons and my daughters are here in Iraq Veterans Against the War.

The war destroys families. The war destroyed my life. I had some problems with Jesus's mother, because when Jesus died and I began to speak out, I began traveling around the country and around the world. I got divorced because the family couldn't understand why I began to change my life. I was cashier. I was newspaper deliverer. I had a job.

But when Jesus died I needed to tell young people that it's necessary to get more education. No more violence. More school, no more weapons, no more bombs. My family didn't understand me and it was destroying for me.

I have had the opportunity to review my life. I have a new wife, but believe me, it's not easy. But this is only one story. Carlos has another story. We have more than four thousand stories now. Five years. How many more stories do you need? How much more blood do the American people need, to stand with the Iraq Veterans Against the War, with the families and say, "Bring the troops home now!" How many more years?

I'm tired. It's been five years. Every single day, I go to schools, I go to the rallies, and I tell the people. But people continue to die, and the children in Iraq continue to die because my government destroyed their lives. My government destroyed my grandson. Please, join together for peace and love. Thanks so much.

NANCY LESSIN AND CHARLEY RICHARDSON,

Son served in Iraq with the 24th Marine Expeditionary Unit of the United States Marine Corps in spring 2003

Founders of Military Families Speak Out

Nancy Lessin

On behalf of Military Families Speak Out (MFSO), we want to say to IVAW what an honor it is to be witness to this profound and historic event, and what an honor it is to work with you in bringing this horrific era to an end. We are your families, and you are our hearts.

In fall 2002, when MFSO was founded, the drumbeats for war were deafening. We noticed that all those who were saying, "We gotta go to war" weren't going anywhere, nor were their loved ones. It was our loved ones who would be sent off as cannon fodder, to kill and die in an illegal, unjustifiable invasion. People said to us, "But your loved ones volunteered." We told them about contracts. Every member of the military signed a contract to defend the Constitution, but the implied vow of the United States government is that you will never be sent into harm's way for no good reason.

We wanted to prevent the invasion for so many reasons. Among them was a deadly equation we learned from the history of this country and from the Vietnam War. Racism plus dehumanization equals horror.

From early on in the invasion, we got e-mails like this one. "My son will be leaving for Iraq within the month. In his last phone call he said he was ready to go over there and kill any Muslim in sight. He even said he'd kill women and children, anyone whose skin is brown. Ironically he's Asian. His skin is very brown. He was calling the Iraqis rag heads. How does a mother respond to that kind of anti-human ranting?"

On November 14, 2003, we asked one of our members if he could write

something for our loved ones and all servicemembers about *not* losing
their humanity. That's how we put it. The next day Stan Goff had written
an open letter to GIs called "Hold onto Your Humanity." It ends this way:

> You are never under any obligation to hate Iraqis. You are never under any
> obligation to give yourself over to racism and nihilism and the thirst to kill
> for the sake of killing, and you are never under any obligation to let them
> drive out the last vestiges of your capacity to see and tell the truth to your-
> self and to the world. You do not owe them your souls. Come home safe
> and come home sane. The people who love you and have loved you all
> your lives are waiting here, and we want you to come back and be able to
> look us in the face. Don't leave your souls in the dust there like another
> corpse. Hold onto your humanity.

We tried to find ways to ask this of our loved ones. MFSO member Rick
Hanson wrote about saying goodbye to his son at the airport:

> I was a father talking to a son with total absence of reference. I had no wis-
> dom to offer; instead, I asked more of him. I asked him to stay focused. I
> asked him not to let his guard down ever. I asked him to do what he was
> trained to do. I asked him to do what he needed to do to survive, and yet
> maintain his moral compass in the middle of it all. I asked my nineteen-
> year-old son to do all of that, and then I apologized as a father for being so
> asleep, for being so cynical and complacent that I let this country send
> him to this war.
>
> In what might have been my next-to-last hug of Eric, I left my tears on his
> right shoulder, as he left his tears on my right shoulder. We held our breath
> for seven, 12, 15, 18 month deployments, back-to-back deployments, third,
> fourth, fifth deployments, stop-loss deployments. The ringing of our phone,
> a knock on the door carried new sinister meanings. We held our loved ones
> close in our hearts, until we could once again hold you close in our arms.

Today MFSO includes almost four thousand military families from across
the U.S. and on bases around the world, many with loved ones now in Iraq.
MFSO also includes families of war resisters. A growing number of MFSO
members are spouses living on bases and in base towns, and there are over
130 Gold Star families, members of our National Chapter, Gold Star Families
for Peace. Their loved ones died as a result of this invasion and occupation.

For those of us lucky enough to have our loved ones come home, all is not well. Every day we get e-mails like this one:

I need your help. My son's body showed up at my house for Christmas, but his mom and I did not know the person who claimed to be our son. He is severely drunk every day, belligerent. He has nightmares every night of the murdered innocent children and Iraqi civilians, and the Army abandoned him as far as giving him help. They will go out of their way to help him reenlist though.

Or this one from MFSO member Stacy Bannerman:

I got my husband back whole physically, and I think his heart is here, too, but I'm not so sure about his mind. He still checks to see where his weapon is every time we get in a vehicle. Although his body is back there is a war that remains between us. I am left to deal with the lost years of time, the lost love of my life. I want to talk with my husband about what he's going through, but I don't have the words. Hell, I don't even have the questions. What's the conversational opener to this: So you inadvertently killed Iraqi children. How's that going for you?... How am I supposed to? How are we?

You already heard from MFSO members Joyce and Kevin Lucey, about their son taking his own life. April Somdahl is also here with MFSO. Her brother, Sergeant Brian Rand, was declared psychologically non-deployable after his second tour in the Middle East, but the army deployed him to Iraq again anyway. He shot and killed himself shortly after returning from that deployment.

There's a line in a poem about the first Gulf War that bears repeating here. It goes, "If I'm sad, how do you suppose that Iraqi mother feels?"

We understand that it's never been a politician who's ended a war. It's always been a social movement. We are proud to be building this movement with IVAW, including this movement inside the military community.

Charley Richardson

This is an occupation that has brought war home and taken its toll on military families. It isolates us from the rest of the nation in our grief, our fear, and our suffering. It enforces a code of silence about an occupation that never should have started, makes us feel alone, and steals our voice. A code of silence remains in effect while the yellow ribbons fade and the magnets fall off the SUVs. A code of silence begins with the troops and extends to their families, and has now been spread to the rest of the nation. The occupation of Iraq has become a war on dissent, particularly dissent within the military community, a war on democracy, and a war on truth.

There are those who say that we as a nation didn't learn the lesson of Vietnam. But unfortunately for all of us, the decision makers did learn the most important lesson: be sure that the vast majority aren't directly affected by the war, and silence the rest with lies and fearmongering. Also, be sure that the sons and daughters of the rich and powerful are not affected or even inconvenienced by the war.

Our so-called leaders have specifically chosen to insulate the majority from the war, and to dump the domestic impact of the war on the troops and their families. They have created a public that despite their opposition to the war is disconnected, distracted, and intimidated.

Sitting here at the National Labor College, I'm reminded of something one of my mentors in the labor movement once told me: that strikes are not won or lost on the picket line. They are won or lost at the kitchen table. The military knows this well. They know that gaining support from the families or at least keeping us silent is critical to keeping this war going. Being called a disgrace to our son was one of the most painful things that Nancy and I have ever experienced, even though we know we are not a disgrace.

The military funds an institute at Purdue University, studying how to keep military families "on the farm." Watch the recruitment ads on television. They're not aimed at the recruits anymore. They are aimed at the families, the ones that need to be convinced. They are working to keep the families silent, and we at MFSO are working to help families find their voice. Every day new families step forward, silent no longer. Together we are building a movement and a community that can support our loved ones in their opposition to the war as well.

While being told by the establishment to be silent, military families are often asked [by the antiwar movement] why our loved ones haven't refused to fight. We are even attacked because our loved ones are in the military, as if the war were somehow our fault. MFSO supports those who have taken stands of conscience and refused to fight, but we also know that it is the citizens of this country who have allowed this administration and Congress to invade Iraq and to keep the war going. It is all of our responsibilities.

The silence of the majority has meant death for the Iraqi people and for our troops. Americans have surrendered their humanity by covering their ears and closing their eyes and going about their daily lives. They have surrendered their humanity by being against the war but not doing anything to end it.

Not one more life. Not one more dime. Not one more lie. End the occupation. Bring the troops home now and take care of them when they get here.

CORPORATE PILLAGING AND THE BREAKDOWN OF THE MILITARY

Former Sergeant Kristofer Goldsmith:
"This is a picture here of me when I
was ten years old wearing all camo,
having a pair of dog tags and giving
my Boy Scout salute. That boy died in
Iraq."   PHOTO: MIKE HASTIE

INTRODUCTION

Through their occupation of Iraq, the Bush administration and Congress are running our military into the ground. Afraid to implement a draft like the one during the Vietnam War, politicians have sent the same soldiers to the front again and again. More than 565,000 Americans have been deployed more than once to Iraq or Afghanistan.[1] In December 2006 the organization *Swords to Plowshares* reported approximately 50 percent of troops in Iraq were enduring their second tour of duty. Another 25 percent were on their third or even fourth tour.[2]

The Pentagon is so stretched that more than forty-three thousand troops listed as medically unfit for combat have been sent anyway.[3] Many of these troops are being redeployed despite surviving a traumatic brain injury, physical brain damage, which is often caused by roadside bombs. Others are being sent to the front despite being diagnosed with Post-Traumatic Stress Disorder, or other severe mental health conditions are being "layered" with PTSD as the horrors of one deployment get caked onto another.

In November 2006 the Pentagon released guidelines that allow commanders to redeploy soldiers with "a psychiatric disorder in remission, or whose residual symptoms do not impair duty performance." The guidelines list PTSD as a "treatable" problem and set out a long list of conditions when a soldier can and cannot be returned for an additional tour in Iraq. Those on lithium, for example, would not be allowed to deploy, while those on another class of medications similar to Prozac may be sent to the front.[4] As of October 2007, the army reports about 12 percent of combat troops in Iraq and 17 percent of those in Afghanistan were taking prescription antidepressants or sleeping pills to help them cope.[5]

This is not only troubling given the stress on the individual servicemember, it's also dangerous for the civilians and other soldiers around him or her. "As a layman and a former soldier, I think that's ridiculous," said Steve Robinson, a Gulf War veteran who works for the organization Veterans for America. "If I've got a soldier who's on Ambien to go to sleep and Seroquel and Klonopin and all kinds of other psychotropic meds, I don't want them to have a weapon in their hand and to be part of my team because they're a risk to themselves and to others."

The army admits the policy is unconventional but maintains it is necessary given the difficultly it's having mustering enough soldiers to continue the occupations of Iraq and Afghanistan. "Historically, we have not wanted to send soldiers or anybody with post-traumatic stress disorder back into what traumatized them," Colonel Elizabeth Ritchie told the *Hartford Courant*. "The challenge for us...is that the Army has a mission to fight."[6]

The length of this war has also caused the Pentagon to continue a policy called "stop-loss," whereupon soldiers are redeployed to Iraq or Afghanistan even after their contract with the military is over. Since September 11, 2001, more than fifty-eight thousand troops have been "stop-lossed," which critics label a back-door draft.[7]

Making matters worse is the fact that many of the soldiers sent to occupy Iraq never imagined they would be sent abroad. Over 250,000 National Guardsmen have been forced to fight overseas in the War on Terror.[8] These men and women who signed up provide emergency help during a flood, earthquake, or civil disturbance are now no longer eligible to do that job, leaving the domestic security of our country at risk.

Military equipment is also breaking down. In March 2007, then-head of the Joint Chiefs of Staff General Peter Pace told a House of Representatives Committee that 40 percent of army and Marine Corps equipment is deployed in Iraq and Afghanistan or being repaired in depots. "It will take end of war plus two years to work off the backlog," Pace told the House Appropriations Defense Subcommittee. "Without being able to give you a [date for the] definite end of war, I can't tell you exactly how long."[9]

All this adds up to a military that is burned out. In the testimony that follows you'll see how that plays out for the soldiers on the ground. American soldiers patrol the streets of Iraq in unarmored Humvees and broken-down Bradley fighting vehicles. When they return, they can't find a military doctor to treat their head injury and then are ordered to deploy for a second, third, or fourth tour. Some see suicide as the only way out.

STEVE MORTILLO

Specialist, United States Army, Cavalry Scout

Deployments: March 2004–February 2005, Fallujah, South of Samara

Hometown: Pennington, New Jersey

Age at Winter Soldier: 25 years old

My troop was awarded the Draper Award for best troop in the 1st Infantry Division. I had the privilege of serving under some very honorable, disciplined, and adept leadership in my immediate noncommissioned officer corps and in my platoon. They're some of the most squared-away and honorable people I think I'll ever meet in my life, and I'll never forget the camaraderie that was shared and the tough times we all went through together. I remember before we left for Iraq standing in formation and my commander at the time came forward and said, "I want everyone to take a moment and I want you to look to your left and to your right and I'm not going to be able to say that everyone that you see to your left and your right will come back, but we're not going to leave anyone behind." At the time it wasn't very real to me. I looked around the platoon and I said, "If there's a group of guys that could make it back without taking casualties this would be the one." I was wrong.

When we got there all our vehicles were pretty much in working order. We had spent some time maintaining them and we started doing what's called presence patrols through Fallujah. We'd roll up and down the street waiting for someone to shoot at us and looking for bad guys dressed the same as all the civilians. At first there wasn't too much going on. People were still wondering what we were doing there and how the occupation was going to manifest.

Around April the violence started picking up. We started getting mortared. We started taking fire from RPGs, IEDs. It's stressful. You're rolling down the road and at any time the ground beneath you can totally disintegrate and you could find yourself dead or—worse—wounded.

I started noticing that there were shortages in some of our equipment, especially track. Track is the equivalent of what tires would be on a car. It's metal track that's linked together with rubber padding designed to cut down on the wear and tear on paved surfaces. Eventually one of the tracks broke and the vehicle flipped on its side and luckily no one was hurt. That's thirty-two tons rolling over; it can do a lot of damage. It came as a surprise to me to see shortages in key equipment when contractors were showing up in the morning hung over, getting paid four times the amount as us. I don't think there's much doubt where the money's going because it's not going to the military.

Around July 2004, I got my leave to go on R&R. When I got back, and I'll never forget this, I was in the reception area and one of my friends pulled me aside and said, "While you were on R&R your platoon leader was hit in the face with shrapnel from an IED." I knew the person; I had done multiple missions with him.

The first thing everyone says is, "Stop lying to me, I don't want to hear that." It was hard for me to accept the fact that he was critically wounded. He had taken some pretty serious damage and the other members of my section had attended to his wounds and initially saved his life. You come back and there's this feeling of guilt that while you were living it up back in the States, one of your comrades got hit, and that was our platoon leader. He was a good platoon leader and he served his men well. He had a lot of respect from us and it was a hard hit to our platoon.

Two or three weeks after that, I was woken up in the middle of the night and informed that another member of my section had been killed by an IED. Again I said, "Quit lying to me, that's not true." It was hard to accept that we had just lost two people from my section in less than a month. He had hit an IED and the Bradley burned to the ground. I mean it's so, it's so.... [breaks down]

Casualties started picking up in my area. The pace of operations started picking up. We started putting a lot more wear and tear on the vehicles. Vehicles started going down. I think at some point there were only two or three vehicles from my platoon that were on line. We were trying to get them in and out of maintenance as soon as possible. But when you're doing six hours on and eight hours off, you have to pull hours of maintenance on your vehicle, clean your weapon, and sleep in that eight-hour time period. You do your best to try to maintain vehicles but eventually they break.

When we were in Kuwait we were told not to set patterns because the enemy would know where we'd be the next day so that they could plan how to attack us. I remember a particular operation called Operation al-Duliyah Sunrise, where we were ordered to do these static checkpoints at the same spot in town over and over again. We didn't receive any contact for two or three weeks. Then in one day we received indirect fire and several people in my troop were wounded, including my medic who was hit in the leg.

The intelligence that we were getting oftentimes seemed to be based on the accounts of just one Iraqi. It would turn out to be a dispute and some-one would come to the American forces and tell us, "Oh so-and-so, he makes bombs, he does this, he does that." And out comes the cavalry, liter-ally, and knocks this guy's door in.

For example, one time we got the order to raid a "bomb-making factory." We pulled up with vehicles and helicopters. We get in the house and it's one guy and the entire building is totally and absolutely empty, and the guy is a painter who's been working on the building, which obviously smells like fresh paint. So we rarely would get someone with weapons or with any kind of proof of guilt. Looking back on it, there's no doubt in my mind that con-tributed to the violence in my area and increased the number of casualties.

On December 21, 2004, my second platoon leader was shot. After that we didn't get another replacement. We were sent on a patrol with limited per-sonnel. If I remember correctly, people had been taken to do "kitchen pa-trol" or washing pots and pans. Mind you, there were contractors on my base and we're going on missions shorthanded. In this instance, it was my-self, a captain, a medic, and one other NCO on a dismounted patrol and we ran into an ambush. We should have had more people that day. I told myself that after I got through this I would be cool and everything would be okay. Just get through this time, I would say, just make sure everyone comes home.

After I got back from Iraq I was diagnosed with Post-Traumatic Stress Disorder. I'll never forget the things that happened over there. I think about them every day and I hope the American people can understand the impact this occupation is having on the United States military. I hope that people educate themselves about the true nature of combat in Iraq and the

Former Specialist Steve Mortillo: "Over many sleepless nights I've made my peace with what I have to do for this country."

PHOTO: MIKE HASTIE

effect it has on our military because it's tearing us apart. In closing, I would just like to say to those who would judge me for coming up here and sharing my experiences with the American people, do so, because over many sleepless nights I've made my peace with what I have to do for this country.

DANIEL FANNING

Sergeant, Wisconsin Army National Guard,
Motor Transport Operator

Deployments: December 2004–December
2005, Convoys all over Iraq

Hometown: Tomahawk, Wisconsin

Age at Winter Soldier: 27 years old

L ike so many others, I enlisted right after September 11, 2001. I joined
out of a sense of duty and patriotism, and wanted to somehow help
and protect the country. I began hearing grumblings about Iraq during my
second year in the military and I immediately had questions like I know a
lot of you did, but I was hesitant to completely dismiss what my president
was saying and what my commanders were saying.

Serving a year in Iraq made me 100 percent confident that the fears and
questions I had before deploying were accurate and maybe it was even
worse than I anticipated. Progress wasn't being made, and the few places
that it was, it simply wasn't worth the cost. The military has had enough.

Within months of our unit returning home we lost two of my good
friends due to mental illness; one was alcohol and the other just reckless
behavior. I know one was seeking support and I imagine since we were
both going through the same VA he was on the same waiting list that I was
on. Two years later, I'm still on that waiting list. Although these names
don't always appear on the evening news and these people don't always die
with full military honors, these are deaths that could have been prevented
just like many in-theater deaths.

For example, when I first arrived in December 2004 our trucks had zero
armor. It was right around that time when a brave specialist named Thomas
Wilson questioned and criticized Secretary of Defense Donald Rumsfeld
about this problem. Our first several missions we had what was affectionately
known as "hillbilly armor": a thin sheet of metal welded onto the sides of our

trucks. It didn't stop bullets. At best it slowed them down. It definitely slowed our trucks down. But once that brave specialist questioned Rumsfeld we all got armor within months. It took a brave soldier to raise that kind of question and to make it a media story. It definitely hurt our morale knowing that it took something like that for the administration to care about us. The same could be said about much of the other equipment we had. The night-vision goggles were a joke. They ran on AA batteries that usually lasted only a couple of hours and we had to shake them every time just to make the batteries work. When we experienced a night ambush outside of Samawa in southern Iraq, we couldn't even see who was shooting at us. I'm not ashamed to admit that instead of trying to fire I was just kind of cowering behind the small armor that I had. You simply couldn't see where your enemy was.

But lack of equipment isn't the only problem that's going on overseas. Regardless of what the Pentagon claims, I was definitely inadequately trained. I spent several hours in basic training learning how to use a bayonet, which is something most people haven't used in combat in several decades. We never received one second of culture or language training. We encountered Iraqis almost daily on the roads, in the marketplaces outside of camps and bases, but we had no idea how to interact with them or how to respect them. Instead while at Fort Benning we received pep talks from well-paid contractors who came into our briefing rooms and insulted the intelligence of the hundreds of us who enlisted voluntarily to serve our country. I remember like it was yesterday, a chubby white guy came into our room. He tried telling us "those liberal tree huggers that are saying this war's about oil are so wrong because we're not importing any oil from Iraq." I mean it doesn't take a lot of research to realize that at the time of the invasion we were getting around 10 to 11 percent of our oil from Iraq. Having people stand before us while in uniform and lie to us hurt our morale.

We weren't allowed to engage with the third-country nationals. They were very low-paid men and women, mostly men from poor countries that the United States hired for next to nothing. We treated them very poorly and disrespected them. They just got cans of food and a few bottles of water for a few weeks' mission. We were told not to assist them but we were responsible for their safety, so that definitely added to our burden as a transportation company because these people came without armor or weapons and most of them didn't know how to speak English or Arabic. I made around $30,000 a year while I was overseas and we'd be passed by the contractors who were making at least three or four times what we were making. We'd see 'em pass by in their black SUVs. They didn't have to follow the same Rules of Engagement that we had and didn't have to engage with the Iraqis the way we did, and that definitely leads to breakdown of the military.

We worked very long and hot days for very long periods of time, and we were almost always on edge. It was very hard to see my best friends break down. It was hard to constantly feel conflicted knowing I was in a situation I didn't want to be in and on a mission that I didn't support. I also knew that I was serving as an unofficial ambassador of the United States and I tried to treat the people that I encountered with respect. I tried to show them that just because our president was a money-hungry warmonger, America was still filled with people who really cared about them and were trying to do the right thing.

I believe the best way we can do that for the Iraqi people is to get out of their way and allow them to start rebuilding their land the way they want. We can and we should help them but our current occupation is doing more to deter that than it is actually assisting.

Lastly, I believe a big reason the military is breaking is because we've lost some of our best members, not only to death and injuries but also because many of us have gotten out. Those of us who enlisted to do what was right but wound up being sent to Iraq—we wound up getting out because we were asked to do what was wrong.

Those who speak against this war are not traitors; we are brave heroes honoring our commitment to this country. Those who wave the flag and have a yellow ribbon on their SUV and claim to support the troops but sit idly by and allow these disgraces to occur have betrayed our troops and betrayed our country. I believe if you truly want to support the troops the best way you can do that is to oppose this war that we never should have been sent to in the first place.

KRISTOFER GOLDSMITH

Sergeant, United States Army,
Forward Observer

Deployments: January–December 2005,
Sadr City

Hometown: Long Island, New York

Age at Winter Soldier: 27 years old

This is a picture here of me when I was ten years old wearing all camo, having a pair of dog tags, and giving my Boy Scout salute. That boy died in Iraq. This is the proud soldier who enlisted just after Christmas in 2003 to support and defend the Constitution of the United States.

I'm from Bellmore, a town in Long Island, New York, twenty minutes out of Manhattan. I could see the smoke when the towers fell on September 11. On September 12 I remember standing up in a pizza restaurant and telling everyone about how I wanted to kill everyone in the Middle East; how the Middle East should be turned into a glass plate by nuclear weapons because that's what I believed. I joined the army to kill people.

I was nineteen years old when I deployed to Iraq and I spent the first eight months of my deployment in the slums of Sadr City. It's a place that was neglected not only by Saddam Hussein but is horribly neglected by America right now. When we went there we promised them freedom; we promised to get them clean water, to get them food, to get them jobs. Instead, there

are two to four hours of electricity a day, randomly. Sewage leaks into their fresh-water system. I never personally saw any contractors working on that water treatment plant outside Sadr City in 2005. My battalion discovered that and reported up and we were told to ignore the fact that nothing was going on. It was a sector that wasn't within our area of operation so don't be concerned with what goes on there.

Imagine living in a place where it gets up to 150 degrees. You don't want to go out during the day, and at night American soldiers are rolling around your streets telling you that you can't go outside, and you can't talk to your friends, you can't enjoy yourself. You can't gather outside the coffeehouse or the *shai* shop because if you go out past dark you're committing a crime. So essentially during the summer months Sadr City was a prison. Three million people in Sadr City were prisoners of war.

I graduated basic training at the top of my class. I graduated warrior leaders course, a leadership development course and noncommissioned officers course, with a 94 percent grade point average. I was a great soldier once upon a time and now I stand here to fight for my brothers more than I ever could while I wore a uniform.

Iraqis unearth a mass grave in May 2005.
PHOTO: KRISTOFER GOLDSMITH

What you see here is civilian Iraqis exhuming bodies of murdered and tortured Iraqis. This was on May 15, 2005, a very hot, uncomfortable, miserable day—I'll never forget it. We don't know why they were killed; we didn't try very hard to find out. We found over a dozen bodies that day.

We weren't authorized artillery, so I became the intelligence reporter and took pictures of these dead bodies. I was told it was so that we could try

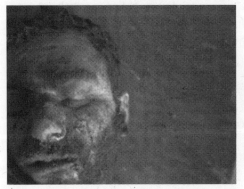

to identify them, but there was no identification process. I never went around to the police stations to post those photos. These photos were never used to help the Iraqis. These pictures were simply trophies of war for people who didn't experience that death. People made videos to send home to their friends and family

In Iraq, Goldsmith's job included taking photographs of dead Iraqis.   PHOTO: KRISTOFER GOLDSMITH

to brag. They were used to build morale, to say that killing is right, death is right, "Dead Iraqis are a great thing," and that's wrong.

While I was taking these pictures I never looked directly at the bodies. I had a digital camera and I held it out in front of me and I looked at the two-and-a-half-inch screen and I flashed that photo. As the flash went off each image was burned into my mind; every one of these pictures is burned into my mind.

The coagulated blood from the man in this photo slinged off his body, off

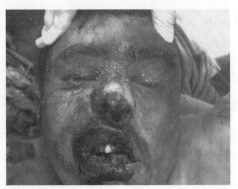

his face onto my shoe. That was the most repulsed I had ever been. There were flies landing on the corpses. They would land on my lips, they would land on my eyes, and they would crawl into my nose. I felt so violated by having been put through this.

I'm reminded of these images when I play video games or walk into a movie.

The coagulated blood of this dead Iraqi landed on Goldsmith's shoe as he took the photo.
PHOTO: KRISTOFER GOLDSMITH

When people ask me, "Hey man, you want to go see *Saw IV* or whatever?" I tell them no, because this is what I see when I watch those movies. This is somebody's brother, this is somebody's husband, this is somebody's son, and this is somebody's cousin. The only reason that we're desensitized to it is because they're not white, they're not American soldiers.

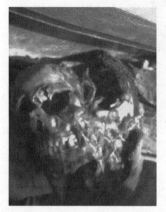

Goldsmith says he didn't want to take this picture, but his command ordered him to.
PHOTO: KRISTOFER GOLDSMITH

That right there: I specifically asked my command, I said, "This man is missing his face, there is no skin left on his head." And they said, "Take the picture anyway." Not to identify him. Whoever was on the other end of the radio just wanted to see the picture, and now because of that person I'm left with that image.

I'd like to read an achievement off of my Army Commendation Medal that I received for my service in Iraq. "While on patrol...in Sadr City, the platoon was called upon to reinforce Iraqi Army battalion in Sector 48. PFC Goldsmith's initiative and timely placement of his weapon system at a key intersection helped...the Iraqi Army battalion...destroy enemy insurgents...without any insurgents escaping the objective."

I'd like to tell you exactly what happened that day. What you heard is true, but what they left out was that I was standing in a Humvee with my platoon sergeant. My platoon sergeant claimed he saw an insurgent and fired upon that man. Because the highest-ranking enlisted man in my platoon fired his weapon, I knew that it was "game on" and I could get away with anything. There was a little boy on top of a building, and he was holding a stick pretending to have an AK-47. He pointed it at me pretending to shoot. I trained my weapon on him and thought, "I hate these Iraqis. I hate these kids who throw rocks and bricks at me. This is my chance; I can kill this kid." Just to take one out of the couple million of 'em out." It took a lot of thinking not to pull the trigger that day. I could have killed a six-year-old boy, someone's son, but I didn't.

When I came home from Iraq all I did was drink. I'm a severe alcoholic and so was just about everybody who lived in the barracks with me. We used to go out every Friday and Saturday night and I would just about finish a 1.75 liter bottle of vodka. I blacked out every time. That was my goal, I wanted to black out. I was self-medicating because we were told that if we sought mental health, we would be locked away and our careers would not advance.

The only thing I looked forward to was getting out of the military and going to college. That hope was taken away from me on January 10, 2007, when George Bush gave his State of the Union address announcing that he was going to send an additional twenty to thirty thousand troops into the sandbox. My unit was one of the five to be locked down with stop-loss. No one could leave—even by reenlisting to go somewhere else to avoid the deployment. People set to retire in two months were locked into an eighteen-month deployment under some of the worst conditions since the initial invasion.

When I found out that I was stop-lossed I went into the sharpest, most anguishing downward spiral that I could imagine. I went into the hospital complaining of chest pain and they had me see a mental health professional. They diagnosed me with depression, anxiety disorder, and adjustment disorder. I was obviously a broken soldier and I was still set to deploy in May 2007, the same week I supposed to get out of the army.

The day before I was set to deploy was Memorial Day. I went out onto a field in Fort Stewart where there's a tree planted for every soldier in the 3rd Infantry Division who's died. I went out among those fallen soldiers and I tried to take my own life. I took pills and my regular poison of vodka and drank until I couldn't drink anymore. The next thing I knew I was handcuffed to a gurney in the hospital. The cops had found me, dragged my body into an ambulance, and locked me up. I spent a week on a mental ward.

After trying to kill myself I was locked up and analyzed and saw doctors, and when I got out of the mental ward I was told that I was going to be removed from the military in a quick, comfortable way. Within two weeks I could be home. The doctors said that I had a severe problem and they recommended removal from service. I was ecstatic. It was great.

Instead, they tried to prosecute me for malingering. My commander, Captain Eric Melloh, who was deployed, decided that I should be removed from the company. I should have my sergeant stripes removed, take money from me, and possibly put me in jail. I went to the military lawyers on Fort

Stewart and asked them to help me help fight this Article 15 nonjudicial punishment, and they said, "No, you need to give up this fight. Because people try to fight it and all it does is bring down the military and blah, blah, blah." I was refused help by the attorneys because they were officers and they didn't want to bring down their own career by supporting me.

I was eventually removed from the military on one of the happiest days of my life, August 16, 2007, on a general discharge. My DD 214, the paperwork, which states every accomplishment of my military service, says in nice big bold letters, "MISCONDUCT, (SERIOUS OFFENSE)." I committed a serious offense by trying to kill myself because I was so damaged by the occupation in Iraq. It was misconduct for me not to deploy while I was handcuffed to a bed in the hospital. So I lost my college benefits, the one thing that really gave me hope. I didn't know where, I didn't know what I was gonna study, but I knew I was going to college in September of '07. That didn't happen. Now I can't pay for it.

My money is disappearing. Between VA visits and personal instability, I've found it extremely hard to find a job. To tell you the truth, I haven't really looked cause I'm having a rough time. So I deliver pizzas on Wednesdays. That's what I am now, a pizza delivery boy. I was a sergeant, I was a leader, I was a trainer, and I was very well thought of. I was a very good soldier. Now I'm a pizza delivery boy who works once a week because that's the only job where I can call in a couple hours before and say, "I'm still at the VA, I'm waiting in line. I'm sorry I can't come in for a couple hours." That is what stop-loss does.

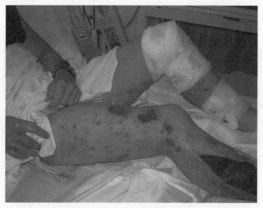

A friend of Goldsmith's, wounded in Iraq.

PHOTO:
KRISTOFER
GOLDSMITH

This man who has to remain nameless is a friend of mine I traveled to North Carolina to see on my way home.

What happened was he stepped on a pressure plate, an antipersonnel mine, and he almost lost his right leg. He had arterial bleeding in his right arm, his left leg, his right leg. He lost all his hearing, ear drum is destroyed in his right ear. This man was supposed to get out of the army the same week that I was, the same week that our unit deployed. So I'm faced forever with "that could have been me" or "if I were there maybe things could have been different." This is someone who was in my platoon, who I served with for a year. When I came into the hospital and I was feeling guilty about trying to kill myself, what this man said to me as soon as I walked into the room was not "Hey how ya doing?" Not "Dude you're a bad person for not coming over there with us." He looked at me with an intense look in his eyes and he said, "Dude you're not going over there right?" And that, that filled my heart with something that no one else could have done.

LARS EKSTROM

Lance Corporal, United States Marine Corps, Assault Man

Deployments: March–September 2005, *USS Ponce*

Hometown: Madison Heights, Michigan

Age at Winter Soldier: 22 years old

Two years ago I would not have believed you if you told me that I'd be standing in D.C. protesting the war. I was very strongly supportive of the war in 2003. I even wore desert cammies in my school photo.

I graduated from high school in 2003. I enlisted in the Marine Corps and went to boot camp that November. After graduating from boot camp and the school of infantry, I felt poorly prepared for battle. Most of the training I received was World War I–style fighting where you're charging across an open field shooting at targets in bunkers with no civilians. Other common training includes patrolling through a two-dimensional forest, firing blanks, or pointing your weapon at other marines with their shirts turned inside out saying, "bang-bang." For most marines that's considered normal training.

Upon arriving at my permanent-duty station, I was attached to the rifle platoon in my company. I then received an extensive urban training, learning how to fast rope out of helicopters, storm buildings, clear rooms, and do legitimate urban fighting.

In this whole eight or nine months of training not once did anyone attempt to teach me to speak Arabic, and I believe our total training as far as dealing with civilians, cultural sensitivity, was about four or five hours at the base theater, receiving speeches on the conduct of war along with other things that no one really paid attention to and we weren't expected to really take to heart and memorize.

As I said, at the beginning of the war I was very pro-war, but events gradually eroded my faith in the military. It started when I was listening to stories from Iraq War veterans. I started to question whether our mission was as clear-cut as the administration had made it seem.

I also noticed incompetence in high places. Throughout our deployment a lot of machine guns and personal rocket launchers were broken or misfired frequently because they were very old. We'd made it as far as Kuwait when an officer noticed that the front sight had broken off one of the Shoulder-Launched Multipurpose Assault Weapons. He was furious and demanded we all sign statements explaining who had it when it broke and why it broke. We had to explain, "Sir, it's been broken for the past year. You didn't notice it during pre-deployment inspection because you were concerned that not everyone had sewn name tapes onto their backpacks and flak jackets."

My personal first aid kit was used during a training mission and I was promised it would be replaced before we deployed. It wasn't. I was issued a nine-hundred-dollar rifle scope without the proper Allen wrench to attach it to the handle of my M-16 so it kept falling off. In its place I used a three-hundred-dollar holographic sight that I purchased with my own money. I've loaned that to another marine who's deploying to Iraq in four days.

All battalions' Humvees were in very poor shape. After Donald Rumsfeld was called out for sending troops to Iraq with unarmored Humvees, all the Humvees were up-armored but they did not upgrade the engines. So you had these very old beater trucks with thousands of pounds of steel bolted to the sides running on dirt roads in Kuwait. We could only go ten to twenty miles an hour even while flooring it. We'd overheat and have to pull to the side.

When I returned from my deployment, I developed chronic depression. After everything had a chance to sink in I was just destroyed emotionally. One day I started crying for hours for no reason. It took my unit months to address my request for psychological help and my depression worsened. I had multiple NCOs and staff NCOs yelling at me for having depression. Just people with the IQ of automated voice machines: "If you require an ass-chewing press 1, if you know someone else who needs an ass-chewing press 2, if you require some sort of empathy or understanding, please hang up and grow a ball sack."

After I'd missed several months of training because of being on light duty for depression, I was instructed by my first sergeant that I either had to get better or take an administrative separation within two weeks. He refused to transfer me to another occupation even though the battalion mail clerk was open and I'd volunteered for it. Because I knew that I wasn't going to get better, I accepted the administrative separation.

I was not allowed to ship my stuff home so I had to give a lot of it away. The morning I received my letter to go home I had to leave within the next couple hours. I was escorted off the base like a criminal and not even given a chance to say goodbye to my friends. After being discharged I was denied benefits from the VA; I've still not received education benefits because I received a general under honorable conditions discharge. I have not heard back from the committee to get it upgraded to full honorable.

I was forced to wait six months after applying for VA benefits for service-connected depression before they would give me any medication or therapy, and at this time I still need to schedule VA appointments approximately one month in advance. And even when I get there it's fifteen minutes of talk, how am I doing: "You want to try new pills? How are the pills you're on now working?"

Lastly I'd just like to say if the president is watching: "The command was uphold and defend the Constitution. Correct yourself!"

LUIS CARLOS MONTALVAN

Captain, United States Army, Armor Officer

Deployments:
September 2003–March 2004, al-Waleed;
March 2005–March 2006, Tal Afar, South
Baghdad

Hometown: Washington, D.C.

Age at Winter Soldier: 34 years old

I n September 2003 I was put in charge of eighty soldiers bound for Iraq deploying to a theater of war with *no weapons*. We traveled into Iraq without *any weapons or ammunition*.Then we were mortared for three days in Balad before arriving in Anbar province for link-up with our unit. How could the greatest army in the world send soldiers into battle without weapons?

Later that month I was put in charge of a key strategic location—the port of entry at al-Waleed, between Syria and Iraq. I was given thirty to forty troopers to secure a hundred kilometers of Syrian-Iraqi border and between five to ten thousand square kilometers of al-Anbar desert. Additionally, we had to secure the enormous border crossing point and recruit, train, and equip Iraqi security forces and redevelop the local infrastructure and economy. I wrote countless memoranda to my superiors requesting more resources and personnel but they went unanswered.

In Iraq I witnessed many disturbing things. I witnessed waterboarding. Two counterintelligence officers stopped a truck full of fake medicine being smuggled into Iraq and brought the driver in for questioning. They lifted his legs. They laid him down. They blindfolded him. Then they lifted his legs again and started pouring water down his throat. After seeing that, I know that's something that we ought not be doing. It's torture.

Separately, I was given unlawful orders by superiors to *not* offer humanitarian assistance to refugees caught between the Syrian and Iraqi borders. I *disobeyed* those orders. I witnessed and participated in countless massive operations led by American commanders whose metrics for success were the number of detainees apprehended. These commanders had no regard for the tribal, ethnic, and sectarian strife caused by American tax-payer–funded militias the U.S. military calls Iraqi security forces.

Most reprehensible was that we never had even close to the amount of troops we needed in Iraq. Yet from 2003 until today Generals Ricardo Sanchez, George Casey, and David Petraeus (among others) did not heed the requests of their subordinate officers for more resources and more troops. Instead, they perpetually painted a rosy picture of the situation while the country fell into civil war. These generals *consistently overstated* the strength and number of Iraqi security forces to Congress and still do. Their misrepresentation of the facts should be grounds for courts-martial and criminal indictments.

I lost many friends in Iraq—American *and* Iraqi. Many Iraqi friends continue to suffer as refugees inside and outside of Iraq. As a matter of fact, an Iraqi friend, whom I consider a brother, fled to Jordan and has been stuck there for two years. As of this testimony, he is meeting with the United Nations High Commissioner for Refugees office in Jordan to process his application for asylum under the United States Refugees Admission Program. My comrades in the U.S. Army and I have sent him letters of support as he frequently risked his life to help us in 2003–04. I pray that Ali and many others are quickly helped.

While at the port of entry at al-Waleed in 2003, I submitted a report to my superiors expressing the need for an automated tracking system for immigration and emigration.

General Ricardo Sanchez and L. Paul Bremer sent a delegation to al-Waleed to assess the installation of a Personal Identification Secure Comparison and Evaluation System (PISCES) to provide tracking of transnational movement. When the team departed, they informed me that the facilities would support the installation of PISCES. By the time I left Iraq in late March 2004, PISCES was not in place.

In 2005 I returned to Iraq for a second tour, as the Regimental Iraqi Security Forces Coordinator. My duties include oversight of the development and security of the northern half of the Syrian-Iraqi border and the border crossing at Rabiya.

In June 2005, Commander Guy Vilardi, working for the Multi-National Corps-Iraq informed me that the Civilian Police Assistance Transition

Team (CPATT) had possession of a dozen PISCES in containers located in Baghdad. He also informed me that they "would install the systems in the near future."

Upon return to western Nineveh province, I informed my superiors that the PISCES were in Baghdad and would be installed soon. In August 2005, General Joseph Fil, commander of CPATT, visited Rabiya to be briefed on the status of the Syrian-Iraqi border. We briefed General Joseph Fil, who scoffed at the notion of installation of the PISCES and stated that "[t]he system is no good and we do not have them anyhow." I informed General Fil of my conversation with Commander Vilardi to which General Fil replied, "[t]hat's not true and the PISCES is no good anyhow."

In January 2006, Colonel Carl Lammers, responsible for Department of Border Enforcement issues at CPATT, sent me an e-mail on a secure network indicating that "the PISCES systems were in fact in containers in Baghdad." I was outraged.

As of March 2006, when the 3rd ACR departed western Nineveh province, no PISCES or equivalent tracking system had been installed at the Rabiya border crossing.

From 2003–2007 no computer systems for tracking immigration or emigration were installed along the Syrian-Iraqi border. This surely contributed to the instability of Iraq. Foreign fighters and criminals were free to move transnationally with little fear of apprehension. It is probable that significant numbers of Americans and Iraqis were wounded or killed as a result.

In January 2007, as a member of American Enterprise Institute's Iraq Planning Group, I discussed this strategic issue. I recommended that PISCES be installed at every border crossing in Iraq *immediately* and that an investigation be launched into how and why this had not yet occurred.

Nearly four years into the war in Iraq and three years after assessing the need for a transnational movement tracking system, no systems had been installed by coalition forces despite having the capability and understanding the strategic necessity. This strategic blunder has yet to be exposed by the mainstream media and no accountability has transpired. I continue to recommend that General Joseph Fil and General David Petraeus be held accountable.

Also in 2005 a very large part of my job was providing logistical support to American and Iraqi units. In that capacity I developed strategies for improving operating procedures and also procuring hundreds of thousands of pieces of equipment. This was essential work as it directly impacted the day-to-day operations of forces serving in very dangerous conditions.

During this time I incessantly tried to get our Division HQ to give us information about the Lee Dynamics International (LDI) warehouse in Mosul. LDI was an American contractor hired by the Department of Defense to provide logistical support to coalition forces across Iraq. The LDI warehouse was the single largest supplier of weapons and equipment for Iraqi police and border police. The personnel involved in that operation were disorganized and utterly incompetent. This directly impacted my ability to do my job and directly affected the lives of thousands of Americans and Iraqis.

After many months of this fraud, waste, and abuse, General Kevin Bergner of our Division HQ took a trip to Baghdad and met with the deputy commanding general of CPATT. I possess a copy of the notes taken between them outlining the lack of accounting practices and operating procedures.

The notes clearly contribute to the compendium against LDI and their gross negligence as contractors in Iraq. LDI should be held accountable for their negligence. I strongly believe that the Department of Defense is covering this matter up to protect senior military leaders. The notes *clearly reveal that neither General Fil nor General Petraeus implemented systems of accounting for millions of taxpayer dollars' worth of equipment and weapons during their tenure in command from 2004–2005.*

General Petraeus, among many other generals and colonels, has been nearly impervious to scrutiny for his failures in Iraq. On the contrary, many of them have been promoted again and again.

Perhaps the greatest lesson this country did not learn from Vietnam was that accountability is essential lest we allow history to repeat itself. Sadly, no generals or administration officials were held accountable then. Ultimately, I believe this is how members of this administration, diplomats, and high-level military leaders got us into the Iraq (and now Middle Eastern) disaster and continue to proctor it with arrogant obstinateness and incredible incompetence.

The "surge" in Iraq was an effort contrived to gain some measure of stability in Iraq while political reconciliation and governing capacity were enhanced. Over one year since the "surge" strategy was proposed, Iraq is no better off than it was. General Petraeus and his "brain trust" of officers and diplomats have made every effort to convince the American and Iraqi people that progress has been made, but the reality is that their metrics are wrought with fallacious assumptions and they offer skewed propaganda.

The government of Iraq is riddled with corruption due to years of American mismanagement and horrible oversight. This is best evidenced in House Committee on Oversight and Government Reform testimony given on October 4, 2007, by former Iraqi commissioner of public integrity, Judge Radhi al-Radhi, who is now in asylum in this country. In his testimony, Judge Radhi spoke about the rampant corruption among U.S. allies, including the Maliki government, and the theft of billions of dollars. He explained that reconstruction had almost stopped, that the lost money was propping up a terrorist movement that was ripping his country apart, and that the current Iraqi government could not be trusted.

In keeping with the spirit and dedication to our nation, for the past year and a half I have authored and co-authored numerous articles with fellow Iraq veterans that have been published in the *New York Times, Washington Post,* and *San Francisco Chronicle,* among other media outlets. The topics have ranged from corruption to complacency and from dereliction of duty to the woeful state of the Department of Veterans Affairs.

I dedicate my testimony today to the life and death of Colonel Ted Westhusing, the U.S. Army's top ethicist and a professor at West Point who volunteered for a deployment to Iraq in 2004. On June 5, 2005, you were found dead from a bullet to the head. Investigations conducted by the army deemed your death a suicide but the circumstances are highly controversial.

In the note, addressed to Generals Petraeus and Fil, found by your body, that the army says is your "suicide note," you stated:

> You are only interested in your career(s) and provide no support to your staff—no [mission] support and you don't care. I cannot support a mission that leads to corruption, human rights abuses and liars. I am sullied—no more. I didn't volunteer to support corrupt, money grubbing contractors, nor work for commanders only interested in themselves.

Duty, Honor, Country…Colonel Ted Westhusing…
Luis Carlos Montalván
Former Captain, U.S. Army

THE FUTURE OF GI RESISTANCE

RONN CANTU

Antiwar soldier Ronn Cantu was promoted to staff sergeant after Winter Soldier: "We do have the right to dissent within the ranks and also serve honorably. My career has not suffered a bit because of anything that I've done in the year and a half that I've been a vocal member of IVAW."

PHOTO: MIKE HASTIE

INTRODUCTION

After more than five years of war, most American soldiers know the same things about Iraq that the American people do: that the invasion of Iraq was based on lies, that there was no link between Saddam Hussein and the 9/11 attacks, and that Iraq had no weapons of mass destruction. Those facts—coupled with the grim, daily reality of life in the war zone—have turned a majority of American soldiers against the occupation.

In February 2006 pollster John Zogby conducted a survey of U.S. soldiers stationed in Iraq. Seventy-two percent said that U.S. troops should be pulled out within one year. Of those, 29 percent said they should be withdrawn "immediately."[1] In other words, if the Bush administration had listened to its own troops instead of implementing the surge, the occupation would already be over.

Servicemembers are coping with this in a variety of ways. Tens of thousands of soldiers and marines have found ways, both legal and illegal, to avoid personally participating in the U.S. occupation of Iraq. The Defense Department reports that 5,361 active-duty servicemembers deserted the U.S. Armed Forces in 2006; nearly thirty-seven thousand defected in the first five years after 9/11. Thousands more have quietly gone AWOL after returning from their first deployment. Three hundred and twenty-five army soldiers have applied to be recognized as conscientious objectors, soldiers who no longer believe in war.[2] Over two hundred have fled the country and are seeking asylum in Canada.

Soldiers who remain inside the military are also fighting back. More than two thousand active-duty servicemembers have signed an Appeal for Redress to Congress demanding an end to the occupation. "As a patriotic American proud to serve the nation in uniform, I respectfully urge my political leaders in Congress to support the prompt withdrawal of all American military forces and bases from Iraq," the petition reads. "Staying in Iraq will not work and is not worth the price. It is time for U.S. troops to come home."[3] The efforts have been endorsed by numerous members of Congress, including civil rights icon John Lewis (D-GA), who released a statement conveying his "deep respect for these men and women and uniform who have taken this courageous and patriotic step.... They have exercised their constitutional right to free speech, and they have questioned an unjust war."[4]

Military blogs have also flourished, both in the United States and in Iraq. Over time, many have developed large followings. Indeed, they have been so successful that in April 2007 the Pentagon was forced to clamp down, requiring all servicemembers to consult a superior "prior to publishing" anything—from "web log (blog) postings" to comments on internet message boards. Failure to do so, the regulations add, could result in a court-martial or "administrative, disciplinary, contractual, or criminal action."[5] As the veterans' testimony at Winter Soldier shows, however, these rules have been impossible to enforce. With limited exceptions, members of the U.S. Armed Forces do not give up their rights to free speech and free expression just because they put on a uniform.

Members of the U.S. military have also begun organizing for better health care and medical benefits and for an end to the U.S. occupation of Iraq. IVAW now has active chapters on bases across America and all over the world—including a growing number of soldiers and marines stationed in Iraq. These efforts are still in their early stages, but as the first wave of servicemembers speaks out, others realize they are not alone and the movement spreads. Five years into this terrible war, the Pentagon's very ability to fight it is becoming diminished.

PHIL ALIFF
Private, United States Army, MOS
Deployments: August 2005–July 2006
Abu Ghraib
Hometown: Atlanta, Georgia
Age at Winter Soldier: 21 years old

Let me begin by saying to my sisters and brothers in Iraq and Afghanistan: You are not alone in your opposition to these illegal occupations. We must struggle together on every military base and in every combat zone and with every veteran to end the occupation. Let me be clear. We have the power to bring the troops home when soldiers throw down their weapons and refuse to fight.

When I joined the military in November 2004, the army and marines were engaged in the second invasion of Fallujah. During my tour in 2006, I was ambushed many times and struck by numerous roadside bombs as my unit fought the insurgency in the farmlands west of Baghdad. This experience radicalized me.

When I returned to Fort Drum in upstate New York I bought a film called *The Ground Truth* and watched it with Sergeant Matt Hrutkay, with whom I served in Iraq. The film inspired Matt to join Iraq Veterans Against the War (IVAW) when he got out of the army. In March of 2007 Matt, along with Vermont veterans, the local Campus Anti-War Network, and members of the International Socialist Organization, put together an event at the Different Drummer Cafe in Watertown, New York. The Different Drummer is the first off-post coffeehouse for GIs since the Vietnam War. It was started by Tod Ensign of Citizen Soldier.

At Different Drummer I met others who articulated an opposition to the war that was in line with my experiences. Three other active-duty soldiers signed up for IVAW, and it gave me a framework for how to organize to end the war. After my rotation at the Joint Readiness Training Center at Fort Polk, Louisiana, I organized a second event at the Different Drummer with former antiwar veterans and civilian activists. We signed up more veterans and built support for Eugene Cherry, a soldier at Fort Drum who went AWOL after returning from Iraq because he was not receiving proper medical treatment for Post-Traumatic Stress Disorder.

As a result of our activism, Eugene avoided a court-martial and was discharged without jail time. It was our first victory at Fort Drum and it built our confidence. If we organized the grass roots to support our struggle, then we could win. Eugene's case also sent a message to the soldiers of Fort Drum that they were not alone.

I met Eli Wright, a combat veteran and medic who had transferred to Fort Drum after serving at Walter Reed and in Iraq. He found the Different Drummer Cafe while walking through Watertown. He had been a member of IVAW for almost two years before coming to Fort Drum. We supported each other in myriad initiatives, all of which were 100 percent legal for active-duty soldiers.

During that time IVAW organized a bus full of veterans to come to Fort Drum. They held barbeques and other social activities and again showed the troops on post that they were not alone. We signed up eight new members and had ninety people from the community come to show their support. This kind of turnout for an event organized by IVAW was a success beyond our wildest imagination.

We began building a model: showing that GI organizing could not be successful without the civilian antiwar movement. In order for soldiers to publicly oppose the occupation, they must have a movement behind them. That is the most important component to the work at Fort Drum. Through our networking with ally organizations we were able to raise money, host events, and make contacts on the base. We worked with every organization that supported our strategy of ending the war.

In the summer of 2007, other IVAW members and I organized a march and rally to publicly introduce our chapter to active-duty soldiers and help the community support war resisters. On September 29, 2007, the march brought over 2,500 people from upstate New York to Fort Drum, and more active-duty GIs became members of IVAW. Within a matter of months, our chapter went from three members to almost thirty.

Because of the high turnover rate within the military, we had to con-stantly train new leaders in the chapter. As soldiers left the military or changed duty stations, they took their experiences from Fort Drum and helped build other chapters around the country. Building a support net-work around the base of experienced organizers was the key to the survival of the chapter because outside organizations helped us develop leadership in our new IVAW members.

As I left the military in early 2008, I was confident in the Fort Drum chapter because we had been successful in building a civilian support net-work, providing outside mental health care for soldiers, and built leader-ship in the chapter that had a focus on base building and growing connections with outside groups in order to inspire soldiers to fight for the end of the occupation in Iraq. Fort Drum was the first active-duty chapter in IVAW and it can be a positive example for the movement.

The most important lesson I learned was that we didn't need to water down our beliefs, nor did we need to shock people into action. GIs are ready for politics. Their experiences are moving them to want a better world, and our ability to articulate our principled opposition to the Iraq war is what gives us the power to end it.

GARETT REPPENHAGEN

Specialist, United States Army, Cavalry Scout, 1st Infantry Division, 3rd Brigade

Deployments:
February 2004–February 2005, Baqouba

Hometown: Grand Junction, Colorado

Age at Winter Soldier: 32 years old

I served as a cavalry scout in the 1st Infantry Division and I went on to go to the Target Interdiction Course in Stetten, Germany, and became a sniper. I served as a sniper for a year in Iraq between February '04 and February '05 around Baquba in the Sunni Triangle.

During our deployment, we started one of the first antiwar MilBlogs, Fight to Survive, and we were involved in a variety of GI resistance but it didn't entail breaking army regulations. That allowed us to receive an honorable discharge. There are ways to resist this war within army regulations.

One of the most important things about our U.S. military is you're a citizen soldier. You retain your rights as a citizen. You're able to use those rights and you should since you're the one sacrificing to protect them. It'll be a shame if the use of the First Amendment becomes unpatriotic.

I joined Iraq Veterans Against the War (IVAW) when they first started out. Myself and the other soldiers I deployed with were resisting before we knew there was an IVAW, before *Sir! No Sir!* or *GI Revolt* came out. When IVAW formed in the summer of 2004, I was contacted by Kelly Dougherty, Camilo Mejía, and some of the other founding members, and as a result, I became the first active-duty member of Iraq Veterans Against the War.

Today we're talking about the future of GI resistance, and you can't help but try to predict the future by looking at the past. I think this Winter Soldier is so incredible. We're doing this far earlier than the Vietnam vets. Thanks to their mentorship, we put this together five years after our invasion and occupation of Iraq. The Vietnam veterans conducted a Winter Soldier in 1971 and the Vietnam War started in 1959; that's more than ten years after the engagement started, and three years after the 1968 Tet Offensive. We had over four hundred thousand American troops deployed in Vietnam at the time. Over fourteen thousand soldiers had been killed in action. I feel that we're ahead of the game. We might be less in numbers and we might have less of a political voice, and America is very different now, but if we can start this resistance early, we can end this war before there is a Tet Offensive in Iraq.

So let's compare Iraq and Vietnam. The military is very different now. When we look at GI resistance, we also need to look at what our military's doing. There's no draft today, so college students are not facing activation. A majority of this war's veterans are still in the military, so the number of veterans isn't as large as it was during Vietnam. These men and women are still stuck in the military through stop-loss orders and the Individual Ready Reserve.

There's a different type of soldier today. They're career soldiers. They're professional soldiers. The men and women that I served with—for many of them that was their career, that was their job, and they took honor in that. They didn't want to give that up. They might not have wanted to go to Iraq or Afghanistan over and over again, but they did take pride in the fact that they were soldiers and they didn't want to lose that. Many of them have wives or husbands and kids that they're trying to support. They thought that the military would be a good way to do that. They didn't ask to be sent to Iraq, to an illegal occupation of another country, and to oppress people who don't want them there. They believed they would be used in a just way, after all peaceful solutions had been exhausted. That's when they thought they'd be sent into harm's way.

Rotations are also different now. Soldiers don't deploy to Iraq one at a time. We're moving entire divisions in and entire divisions out. The men that I served with are the same men I served with when I was in Kosovo. They are the same men I trained with in Germany. We are loyal to one another. Many of these men and women feel that the military is their family, and they don't understand civilian life. They're comfortable in the military and they don't want to abandon their friends and family, but that doesn't mean that they want to serve, repeatedly, in Iraq.

There are many benefits available to these men and women. They're offered GI bills for college. They're given health insurance. They're given a nice safe base to live on where their spouses can shop at the PX or the commissary. Their kids are going to school in a safe, healthy environment, and that's hard to give up as well.

So when you ask why don't soldiers resist, these are all these reasons why they don't. Many of them are scared as hell to be in the outside world when all they've ever been is a machine gunner.

The three reasons soldiers continue are the benefits, the options, and the loyalty to and pride of service. But there are solutions to each. We can start funds to help war resisters replace military benefits. We could hire veterans. We could give them jobs and someplace to land once they decide to turn their back on this war.

They can also join this movement. There's a lot of pride and loyalty in joining our army and our Corps and in fighting for a cause we believe in, fighting for a cause that will change America and stop these occupations.

So we're asking. We're not going to come out and recruit soldiers or veterans. We're not going try to trick you into joining us and to joining our cause. But we will ask you to. Because there is a fight coming, and it's a fight to improve America and to improve this military and we're asking you to join us.

So if you're out there and you're dedicated to what we're talking about here at Winter Soldier and you want to improve your military and your country, this is a good way to do it. Go to http://www.ivaw.org and there's membership applications online.

We'll give you information on how you can resist if you want to stay in the military and you don't want to break army regulations. If you don't want to get in trouble, there are still ways you can use your First Amendment rights. You can put your application in and join us to end this occupation.

RONN CANTU

Staff Sergeant, United States Army,
Interrogator

Deployments:
February 2004–March 2005, Fallujah;
December 2006–January 2008, Baghdad

Hometown: Los Angeles, California

Age at Winter Soldier: 30 years old

For the record, nothing I say should be construed to be the opinion of the Department of the Army, the Department of Defense, or the United States government.

I left the military shortly after 9/11. It was the end of my four-year contract. I felt like I left the country when it needed me most, and so when I watched America build a case for the Iraq war, I fell for it hook, line, and sinker. I was in school when the war broke out, and I tried desperately to finish my semester, but in late March 2003 I was in that recruiter's office again saying, "You gotta make me a part of this, you have to get me over there." And it was just timing, but the quickest they could get me out was August 2003. In May 2003, mission was "accomplished," and I was like, "Great." There was my story for my grandkids: I missed my chance for some honor.

But soldiers were still dying. And so when I got to my duty station in Germany in September 2003, I found out I would deploy to Kuwait in February 2004. But in December 2003, Saddam Hussein was caught, so for the second time I thought, "Great, now the war is really over." But we still went, and by that time I was extremely skeptical. Over the course of that year, I felt the same frustration that everybody did. I didn't realize that the war was over and that the occupation had begun.

And so the only thing we were fighting for was living one more day. The frustration is that no matter what you do, you're not going to get home any sooner. Then I felt the frustration of coming home and having to con-

stantly remind myself that America's a country at war because you would-
n't know when you look around.

In between tours I had time to think about the things that I had done.
How we went to Iraq under false pretenses. How I went there to help the
Iraqi people and that's not what we were doing. It wasn't malice; we were
just trying to survive. I started to blame the Iraqi people for our presence,
and I *did* want to see Iraq annihilated. I just wanted to go home. It was
what all of us wanted back then, and it was every bit as true in 2007.

I thought I would tell a story of how the First Amendment really came
to bat for me. I joined IVAW right before my second deployment. I started
writing posts that got published on the site, and it started getting attention
because here was this active-duty soldier getting ready to go on his second
deployment. I was contacted by a reporter while I was in Baghdad. He said
he was with *Democracy Now!* I had never heard of it before, but I agreed to
an interview on so-and-so date. It just so happened that on that date I was
going to be investigated for something entirely different.

I had a website, www.soldiersvoices.net, that I didn't register with Central Command. It's policy to register all blogs and websites and I had failed
to register this one—and they had found it.

I didn't know I was going to be investigated until that day, and I remember I was in my commander's office answering questions when my phone
started ringing. I was like, "Oh, man." She wanted to know who that was,
and I said, "It's a reporter."

She gave me a direct order not to talk to the media. Now, this reporter
was calling me one hour before the show was supposed to broadcast live.
The phone rang constantly. I didn't answer it and then it stopped. And I
was like, "Great, they just got the hint." And after I was done, my phone
rang again and I answered it, and he's like, "Do you still want to do this? We
go on in ten minutes." And I said, "I don't think I should. I've just been
given a direct order not to speak to the media." And he's like, "How 'bout if
I just give you thirty seconds to say what you have to say to the American
people." And I said, "I can work with that." So I had five minutes to come
up with thirty seconds to say, and he called and he's like, "I'm gonna put
you on right now." I can hear somebody talking and she wasn't talking to
me. I thought to myself, "Oh, God, is this live?"

So she's like, "Ronn are you there? Would you...." She started asking me questions and I blew her off. I just blew through my thirty-second blurb in about five seconds.

After a few questions, I hung up the phone. I'm like, "Oh, that's done." And ten minutes later somebody found me and said, "The commander wants to see you in her office right now." I was sad because I was I thought I was going to jail and I was upset because, having gone to school in America, I thought, "That's not what this country was supposed to be about. All I did was say things I felt had to be said." I knew IVAW existed and I had just joined, but I hadn't met anybody yet, and I was wary of anything labeled antiwar at the time because I've got so many years of military experience.

So I said, "I'm not going take this laying down." I went in there fully prepared for a confrontation. I shed a tear or two, and I went in there and she said, "I'm rescinding my order for you not to talk to the media. It is, in fact, your right."

It was sink or swim time. At best I treaded water and I came out ahead. It is our right, and I want the servicemembers and my active-duty brothers and sisters to know that is our right. We do have the right to dissent within the ranks and also serve honorably. My career has not suffered a bit because of anything that I've done in the year and a half that I've been a vocal member of IVAW. And I just want to say that I know that you guys are out there. There's IVAW in every unit, on every post in the military. Even if you're not IVAW members, I know that you're Iraq veterans and you are against this war.

To everybody else, I want to say please don't let us be the first generation of veterans to be forgotten while our war is going on. When you have to look hard for news on Iraq, it really sends a powerful message to us still on active duty.

Finally, I just want to give myself a little shout-out. Today is my thirtieth birthday. The reason I wanted to say that is I'm doing this for the soldiers over there right now so they could one day see thirty as well.

CONCLUDING REMARKS FROM CAMILO MEJÍA

Chair of the Board, Iraq Veterans Against the War

Camilo Mejia served in Iraq from April through October 2003. He was the first soldier to be incarcerated for publicly refusing to return to Iraq. He currently serves as the chair of the board at IVAW and is the author of Road from ar Ramadi: The Private Rebellion of Staff Sergeant Mejia: An Iraq War Memior.

George Orwell once wrote, "In times of universal deceit, telling the truth becomes an act of rebellion." We live today in times of universal deceit, but here at Winter Soldier, we have witnessed firsthand accounts that challenge that universal deceit.

Iraq Veterans Against the War has become a source of stress to the military brass and to the government. We have members who have been interrogated by the FBI, who have been incarcerated for being conscientious objectors and for saying no to command rape and sexual discrimination. We have members in Iraq Veterans Against the War who have been prosecuted for criticizing our government's failed war policies.

We have become a dangerous group of people not because of our military training, but because we have dared to challenge the official story. We are dangerous because we have dared to share our experiences, to think for ourselves, to analyze and be critical, to follow our conscience, and because we have dared to go beyond patriotism to embrace humanity.

The servicemembers and veterans who have shared our experiences with you and with the entire world are committing an act of resistance by being here. We resist the notion of free speech and democracy when the voices of those who have been the most affected by the occupations of Iraq and Afghanistan are being silenced by the government and by the corporate media.

We refuse the notion of nation building in Iraq when at home our levees are breaking and our people are drowning, and when our own bridges are falling down. We resist and reject the official government rhetoric of "Support Our Troops" when we have a whole new military generation returning home to no care for Post-Traumatic Stress Disorder, to homelessness, to disturbingly high levels of suicide, homicide, and domestic violence. We have heard heartbreaking testimony. We who have been there have seen the horror in the eyes of children whose doors we kicked down at 3:00 in the morning.

We cannot win the hearts and minds of any country until we win the hearts and minds of our own people, until we eradicate homophobia within our ranks and we treat our own people as equals regardless of their gender or the color of their skin.

You have heard our three points of unity: immediate and unconditional withdrawal of all occupying forces, full benefits to all military personnel, and reparations to the people of Iraq so they can rebuild their country on their own terms. We at IVAW are not going to rest until we achieve these three goals.

I first became an activist, home on a two-week leave from Iraq, in October of 2003. At first I simply contradicted reporters when they claimed that morale was high among the troops. Then I started talking about how we were going out there on combat missions without basic equipment, such as bulletproof vests and radios. For lack of armored plates on our vehicles we had to line their walls with old flak vests, their floors with sandbags. I told reporters that in some cases we had to ask other platoons to give us some of their munitions before going out on patrols. And sometimes patrols would get cancelled because we didn't have but two bottles of water per soldier at a time when the temperature was reaching 140 degrees.

My speaking out then became more radical after I decided I would not return to my unit in ar Ramadi at the end of my R&R leave. I began to speak about the torture of prisoners and the killing of civilians. By the time I surrendered, five months after the end of my leave, I was calling the occupation illegal and immoral and saying servicemen and women did not have a duty to fight in it. The army convicted me of desertion and put me away for nine months.

I started working on GI resistance shortly after I was released from prison in February 2005. I officially joined IVAW the following month and I have been a full-time activist ever since. Over the past several years, I've been asked over and over how come the antiwar movement is not as strong as it should be. The answer to that question is complicated and can only be found in an analysis of the political and historical context surrounding the Vietnam War. Such an analysis would note that back then there was a draft that touched the sons of the U.S. middle class, which unleashed the outrage of the more affluent ranks of society, culminating in draft resistance, mass desertions and conscientious objector applications, a militant antiwar student movement on hundreds of college campuses, and massive street demonstrations. Another aspect from that era missing in today's movement is the fresh legacy of the civil rights movement. Young recruits and members of today's military don't have that point of reference, or even that of resistance to the Vietnam War. That history has been removed from the official records in order to disempower new generations of activists.

Yet another disadvantage of today's movement is the lack of personal engagement of the American public, which is explained not only by the fact that fewer than half a percent of the population is directly involved in the fighting, but also by the fact that those fighting belong to the less affluent sectors of society: working Americans, people of color, immigrants, the uninsured and uneducated; in short, people with lots of needs but very little socioeconomic power.

Today's society is not experiencing the horror that our military intervention of Iraq is causing to both Iraqis and to servicemembers and their families. Hiding the gruesome reality of the occupation of Iraq is not meant to respect the dignity of the fallen, as our government would have us believe. It is meant to minimize the emotional impact of the occupation so that the United States, as a nation, does not take ownership of the crimes the government commits in its name, with its money, and with the blood of its sons and daughters.

Part of the work of GI organizers is to ensure that the American people, through the voices of veterans and active members of our military, *do* experience the war. We want regular civilians to know about the suffering of Iraqis, and how our military operations are carried out in the countries we occupy. We want the public to know that occupation translates into the oppression of people, into the killing of unarmed Iraqi civilians, into the humiliation of an entire nation, into the destruction of the environment, and into the destruction of the moral fabric of the members of our military.

In order to achieve this goal, to help the American people take ownership of the actions of our government and of our military, we have to empower our brothers and sisters, both veterans and active-duty and reserve personnel, to speak out. We want people at home to hear not from the government pundits, officials, generals, or from the politicians, but from those of us who have intimate knowledge of our military and of war and occupation.

During the Vietnam era the work of those organizing GIs to speak out was aided by news reports, which were actually depicting the horror of war. Even as someone who was not born in that era, I have imprinted in me some of the horrific images that came from that war: the little Vietnamese girl running toward a television camera, naked, as the village behind her is being bombed with napalm. There were pictures of American soldiers posing with dead Vietnamese as if they were war trophies. There were the images of our own wounded, of our dead, and of those who were alive in body but who were also dead in spirit. The demoralization of our military was able to penetrate into the consciousness of the American public. People in the United States were able to take a peek into the hell of war, a hell that we were unleashing on the people and on the land of Vietnam and that was being carried back home in the hearts of our veterans.

The hell that's being brought back from Iraq and Afghanistan is being kept from the American public this time around. This means that today's GI resistance movement has to do double the work in order to help regular people realize the huge burden of the occupations of Iraq and Afghanistan, and that this is their burden too. The American people have to take ownership of these occupations; that's the only way they're going to get out there and protest, not as a favor, but because it affects them personally and because they have a moral responsibility to put an end to the atrocities. Ending the occupations is not a battle that antiwar GIs should have to wage by ourselves. It is not a burden we should bear alone.

The need to empower our brothers and sisters in the military to speak out serves several purposes. On one hand it sends the message to other service personnel that they're not alone in their opposition to the occupations and that they *can* and *should* take a stand. On the other hand it brings the horror of war into the consciousness of regular Americans at a time when the mainstream news outlets are going out of their way to hide that horror.

We in the GI resistance movement want to put a human face to the suffering of Iraqis and Americans alike. What does it mean to the newspaper reader when on the lower inside corner of page A18 he or she reads that three American personnel were killed in an IED attack? How much of the pain felt by the families of those three military personnel can be conveyed by that little box? And what about the Iraqi casualties, the children, the wives and mothers, the fathers, and the destroyed homes—who speaks for them in America? And what about the survivors, who return home with the images of so much suffering forever branded in their hearts?

Winter Soldier Iraq and Afghanistan, chronicled in this present volume, is the biggest, most important event ever put together by Iraq Veterans Against the War. Modeled after the Winter Soldier hearings held by Vietnam Veterans Against the War (VVAW) in a Detroit, Michigan hotel in 1971, Winter Soldier Iraq and Afghanistan did not start a new tradition; rather it added a new chapter in the rich history of military resistance that dates back to the Revolutionary War and that carried through to this very day, finding its highest and most successful expression in the military resistance to the Vietnam War.

Without the experience, support, and mentorship of VVAW and Veterans For Peace (VFP), Iraq Veterans Against the War would be walking down very dark roads as we move forward. We know from the experience of our mentors that the government, bent on continuing its criminal wars of aggression at all cost, will persist in trying to isolate the critical voices within the ranks. The history has been rewritten to portray the antiwar movement of the '60s and '70s as anti-military. But we know from our mentors at VVAW that the military, like today, was at the forefront of the resistance: distributing hundreds of GI newspapers, opening GI coffeehouses right outside of military bases, organizing veterans and active-duty GIs, and staging huge antiwar rallies, marches, and speakouts.

In Vietnam entire units were refusing to go on missions that were not worth their lives. They began telling their officers how missions would be carried out in order to minimize unnecessary danger. They practiced search-and-avoid missions and went as far as negotiating unofficial truces with their so-called enemies, which they accomplished by wearing white armbands around their sleeves, among other signs.

Today's military resistance is not as advanced as that of our Vietnam predecessors, but the signs of an ever-escalating disaffection among the ranks, both on the battlefields and at home, become more palpable each passing day.

Sharing our experiences as veterans and as human beings during the Winter Soldier hearings has not only given voice to those of us who will no longer stand quiet in the face of these criminal occupations, it has also brought us together and returned to us the sense of family we were looking for when we joined the military. If our military experience at war has taken from us our humanity, having been able to testify at Winter Soldier renewed in many of us the hope of finding a new life in resistance.

The Iraq War was launched under false pretenses and in direct violation of American and international law. As servicemembers we have a duty to resist participation in illegal wars and to disobey unlawful commands. Torture, the indiscriminate killing of civilians, and conducting combat missions in certain civilian areas are all illegal orders that should be refused. But the government would have people believe that these are the actions of a few bad apples and not the result of policy crafted at the highest spheres of power.

These Winter Soldier testimonies, provided by servicemen and women from different branches of the military, who served at different times and in different places and who for the most part did not know one another until joining IVAW, point to a systemic problem that can only end when the occupations themselves end. People in the antiwar movement sometimes make the argument that if we leave Iraq will fall into absolute chaos, but the testimonies we provide in this book show how there is already chaos in Iraq, and how that chaos is caused by the occupation itself.

Saying that because "we broke it we have to stay until we fix it" fails to explain how certain things, once broken, can never be fixed again. It also does not convey the idea that broken things can get even "more broken." In the case of the occupations of Iraq and Afghanistan we are not simply talking about "things," we are talking about human lives and human dignity. A woman who loses her little boy to our bullets will carry a wound that can never be fixed. But if the occupation continues so does the possibility that the rest of her family can also be killed by our bullets—we don't stay in her country to "fix her." We can't do that. We stay in her country to cause further damage, to deepen her wound, to inflict new ones, and to perpetuate the cycle of violence that destroys nations.

By providing our testimony we hope we can help people understand why we demand an unconditional and immediate withdrawal of all occupying forces from Iraq. We hope people can see that we demand full benefits for all servicemembers and veterans because without those benefits many of our brothers and sisters simply will not survive (and many are losing the battle every day). We want people in the United States to see how our military presence in the Middle East is responsible for the untold suffering of millions and to understand why we demand that our government pay reparations to those people.

Perhaps our motive for bringing our brothers and sisters home is a bit selfish, but not in a bad way. We stand for justice for the people of Iraq and for our own people because in order to live with ourselves we have to take that stand. Our survival depends on it.

We in the GI resistance movement cannot rely on the electoral process or on the promises of elected politicians because we cannot afford to be demoralized. While politicians and an entire new Congress get elected on antiwar platforms the occupations continue, as do the destruction, the killing, and the unnecessary bloodshed of innocent people in Iraq and Afghanistan.

As we empower other members of the Armed Forces and other veterans to stand up for what they believe in by speaking truth to power, we want to send the clear message both to the government and to the larger antiwar movement that we will not stop our efforts to organize GI resistance until all of our demands are met. We know the only way wars and occupations can continue indefinitely is when members of the military fail to question their leadership and continue on fighting and obeying clearly illegal and immoral commands.

GI, you don't have to do that.

I hope the book before you has conveyed a bit of the horror we live with, as well as the conviction that ending the occupations of Iraq and Afghanistan is the right and moral thing to do. We know because our work to end the occupations is where we draw the energy to live every day, and because through that work we are able to rebuild ourselves and find new life. We are here. And we are not merely survivors. We are fighters. We are Winter Soldiers.

AFTERWORD

Aaron Glantz

The veterans who spoke at Winter Soldier could have stayed silent. They could have accepted parades and accolades of heroism and blended back into society and the world would have never known about the terrible atrocities they committed or witnessed in Iraq and Afghanistan. By coming forward to share their stories, however, these veterans have done a great service, permanently changing the historical record of "what happened" in the war zones.

I will never forget Winter Soldier as long as I live. As a journalist who's spent the last six years covering the Iraq War, first from Turkey and Jordan, then from Iraq, and then back here in the United States, I've never heard any words from anyone in this country that struck me as closer to the truth. Usually Americans talk about war like it's a Nintendo game or a series of lines and arrows on a map. Elites from the left and right talk about the American soldiers and Iraqi people like they are chess pieces to be moved around for the maximum benefit of a particular cause or ideology. Nobody stops to talk about what is *actually happening*, because the pain and suffering of those on all sides is uncomfortable and almost beyond comprehension—even for those of us who have witnessed it personally.

Four months after Winter Soldier, the words of former marine Jon Michael Turner still ring in my mind. "The reason I am doing this today is not only for myself and for the rest of society to hear. It's for all those who can't be here to talk about the things that we went through, to talk about

the things that we did," he said. "Until people hear about what is going on
with this war, it will continue to happen, and people will continue to die."

When I was in Iraq, I worked as an unembedded journalist. I had no military escort. I traveled around in taxis and beat-up old economy cars and
met regular Iraqi people and talked with them about their daily lives and
their attitudes about the U.S. occupation. My biggest safety concern was not
the "insurgents" but the American soldier at a checkpoint with an itchy trigger finger and loose Rules of Engagement. On my first day in Iraq in April
2003, at the first checkpoint I crossed, a young soldier with a helmet too big
for his head almost lit me up when I stepped out of the taxi. The only thing
that saved me was that I was with another journalist…and he was blond.

Over my three trips to Iraq from 2003 to 2005, I reported stories that
were eerily similar to those presented by veterans at Winter Soldier. In Fallujah, I watched a medical team lift the rotting corpse of a middle-aged
woman out of the garden of a neighbor's home. In Babylon, I visited a
human rights office that had been raided by the U.S. military, parts of two
sheiks' brains splattered on a hallway wall. West of Baghdad, I spoke with a
tribal chief whose sons had been pulled over by U.S. soldiers at a checkpoint and then thrown off a bridge into the Tigris River to their deaths.

As I reported these stories, my heart filled with rage at these Americans
and I felt myself going through the same process of dehumanization the
veterans described at Winter Soldier. If I had a weapon instead of a micro-
phone, I don't know what I would have done. I understood the motiva-
tions of the fighters who fired on the American soldiers as they rolled their
tanks and Humvees through civilian neighborhoods. I returned home
with a rage toward these soldiers and toward my country, a rage that has
only subsided after I've had the opportunity to meet these same soldiers
now that they're veterans and have had the chance to take off their uniforms and put down their weapons. I've understood through these personal interactions that in war it is not the "other side" that is the enemy but
the war itself and the leaders who started it.

This is why I think Winter Soldier is so important. These brave veterans,
by coming forward en masse and in public, give us the opportunity to
begin an important conversation about the nature of war and the effect on
the human condition. Someday soon this war will end and the last American troops will come home from Iraq. At that point American veterans and

Iraqi civilians will be able to sit across the table from each other without guns, tanks, or mortars and have the same kind of exchanges that each of us do with our neighbors.

During my three trips to Iraq I was met with great courtesy by nearly every Iraqi I encountered. Across the country, Sunni, Shia, and Kurdish families all invited me into their homes and offered me tea and sometimes a complete lunch. It didn't matter that I was an American. The main point was that I was interested in their story and didn't carry a gun. Iraqi people are ready to have this conversation and Winter Soldier shows American veterans are too.

June 13, 2008

NOTES

Introduction

1. "Valley Forge Encampment: A Winter of Suffering," National Park Service, available at: http://www.nps.gov/history/logcabin/html/vf.html.
2. Gerald Niccosia, *Home to War: The History of the Vietnam Veterans Movement* (New York: Crown Books, 2001), 80.
3. "Flashback: A Rare Broadcast of John Kerry's 1971 Speech Against the Vietnam War Before the Senate," *Democracy Now!*, July 30, 2004, available at: http://www.democracynow.org/2004/7/30/flashback_a_rare_broadcast_of_john.
4. "Opening Remarks to the Senate Armed Services Committee," General George Casey, February 28, 2008, available at: http://www.army.mil/-speeches/2008/02/28/7824-opening-remarks-house-armed-services-committee/.

Rules of Engagement

1. *Off Target: The Conduct of the War and Civilian Casualties in Iraq*, Appendix E, "The Rules of Engagement for US Military Forces in Iraq," Human Rights Watch, December 2003, available at: http://www.hrw.org/reports/2003/usa1203/index.htm.
2. Colin Kahl, "In the Crossfire or the Crosshairs: Norms, Civilian Casualties, and US Conduct in Iraq," *International Security* 32, No. 1 (Summer 2007): 4–46.
3. Josh White et al., "Homicide Charges Rare in Iraq War: Few Troops Tried For Killing Civilians," *Washington Post*, August 28, 2006, A01.
4. A full database of these internal Pentagon documents is available on the website of the American Civil Liberties Union, http://www.aclu.org/natsec/foia/search.html.
5. Gilbert Burnham et al., "Mortality After the 2003 Invasion of Iraq: A Cross-sectional Cluster Sample Survey," *The Lancet*, October 11, 2006.

Racism and the Dehumanization of the Enemy

1. "President Bush Meets with Alhurra Television on Wednesday," The White House, May 5, 2004, available at: http://www.whitehouse.gov/news/releases/2004/05/20040505-5.html.
2. Jennifer Harper, "'Bad News' Rife in Military Coverage," *Washington Times*, June 14, 2006.
3. Noel Cisneros, "San Jose Marine Granted Conscientious Objector Status," April 1, 2007, available at http://abclocal.go.com/kgo/story?section=news/local&id=5173724.
4. Aaron Glantz, "Civilian Court Sides with Conscientious Objector," Inter Press Service, April 5, 2007, available at http://ipsnews.net/print.asp?idnews=37233.
5. S.L.A. Marshall, *Men Against Fire* (New York: William Morrow Company, 1950) 54–58.
6. David Grossman, *On Killing: The Psychological Cost of Learning to Kill in War and Society* (Boston: Back Bay Books, 1996) 252–54.
7. Philip Zimbardo, *The Lucifer Effect: Understanding How Good People Turn Evil* (New York: Random House, 2007) 307–308.

Civilian Testimony: The Cost of War in Iraq

1. International Committee of the Red Cross, "Iraq: No Let-Up in Humanitarian Crisis," March 2008, available at: http://www.icrc.org/web/eng/siteeng0.nsf/htmlall/iraq-report-170308/$file/ICRC-Iraq-report-0308-eng.pdf.
2. Refugees International, "The Iraqi Displacement Crisis," March 3, 2008, available at: http://www.refugeesinternational.org/content/article/detail/9679.
3. "Iraq Poll March 2008," D3 Systems of Vienna, VA, and KA Research Ltd. of Istanbul, Turkey for ABC and *BBC News*, available at: http://abcnews.go.com/PollingUnit/Story?id=4444000&page=4.
4. Ciara Gilmartin, "The 'Surge' of Iraqi Prisoners," (Washington, D.C.: Foreign Policy in Focus, May 7, 2008), available at: http://fpif.org/fpiftxt/5207.
5. Translation in English: "Thank you very much for being here today. God willing, we will go together to Iraq someday and share in happiness and security. Today, we will talk about the situation in Iraq."

Divide and Conquer: Gender and Sexuality in the Military

1. Sara Corbett, "The Women's War," *New York Times,* March 18, 2007.
2. Helen Benedict, "Women Warriors," *International Herald Tribune*, May 26, 2008.
3. Ibid.
4. Helen Benedict, "The Private War of Women Soldiers," Salon.com, March 7, 2007, available at: http://www.salon.com/news/feature/2007/03/07/women_in_military/.
5. National Center for Post Traumatic Stress Disorder, *Iraq War Clinician Guide: Military Sexual Trauma*, 66–67, available at: http://www.ncptsd.va.gov/ncmain/ncdocs/manuals/iraq_clinician_guide_ch_9.pdf?opm=1&rr=rr1519&srt=d&echorr=true.

6. "Arguments for Repealing Don't Ask, Don't Tell," Servicemembers' Legal Defense Network, available at: http://www.sldn.org/binary-data/SLDN_ARTICLES/pdf_ file/3195.pdf.
7. Michael Boucai, "Balancing Your Strengths Against Your Felonies: Considerations for Military Recruitment of Ex-Offenders," February 13, 2007, Michael D. Palm Center at the University of Santa Barbara, available at: http://www.palmcenter.org/ files/active/0/boucaiM_strengthsFelonies_092007.pdf.
8. Army Regulation 601-201, pages 35–36, available at: http://www.palmcenter.org/ files/active/0/Army_Regulation_601-210.pdf.

The Crisis in Veterans' Health Care and the Costs of War at Home

1. Ira Katz, "Re: Suicides," e-mail to Michael J. Kussman, Undersecretary of Health, Veterans Administration, December 15, 2007, Plantiff's Exhibit P-1283, United States District Court for Northern California, Case No., C 07 3758.
2. Ira Katz, "FW: Not for the CBS News Interview Request," e-mail to Ev Chasen, VA Spokesperson, February 13, 2008, Plaintiff's Exhibit P-1269, United States District Court for Northern California, Case No., C 07 3758.
3. Ibid.
4. "The Truth About Veterans' Suicides," Hearing of the House Committee on Veterans Affairs, May 6, 2008. Transcripts and video of the hearing available at: http://veterans.house.gov/hearings/hearing.aspx?NewsID=237.
5. Veterans for Common Sense v. Peake, Northern District of California Before the Honorable Samuel Conti, Trial Transcript Final, April 30, 2008, 1369, 1372.
6. Department of Defense: Iraq War (Operation Iraqi Freedom, OIF), Casualties from March 19, 2003, through May 31, 2008; DoD Contingency Tracking System, through March 31, 2008; and Afghanistan War (Operation Enduring Freedom, OEF), Casualties from October 7, 2001, through May 31, 2008.
7. Department of Veterans Affairs, "Analysis of VA Health Care Utilization Among US Global War on Terrorism (GWOT) Veterans," March 25, 2008, and "VA Benefits Activity: Veterans Deployed to the Global War on Terror," April 16, 2008. Obtained by VCS using the Freedom of Information Act.

The Breakdown of the Military

1. "CTS Deployment File Baseline Report for Operating Enduring Freedom and Operating Iraqi Freedom as of October 31, 2007," Defense Manpower Data Center, obtained by Veterans for Common Sense using the Freedom of Information Act.
2. Amy Fairweather, Risk and Protective Factors for Homelessness among OIF/OEF Veterans (San Francisco: Swords to Plowshares, 2006).
3. Greg Zoroya, "US Deploys More than 43,000 Unfit for Combat," USA Today, May 8, 2008.
4. Leo Shane, "New Guidelines Allow Troops Who've Recovered from Traumatic Stress Disorders to Redeploy," Stars and Stripes, December 22, 2006.

5. Mark Thompson, "America's Medicated Army," *Time*, June 5, 2008.
6. "Mentally Unfit, Forced to Fight," *Hartford Courant*, May 17, 2006.
7. Rick Maze, "Bill Would Pay Extra for Stop-Loss Service," *Army Times*, May 25, 2008.
8. "CTS Deployment File Baseline Report for Operating Enduring Freedom and Operating Iraqi Freedom as of October 31, 2007," Defense Manpower Data Center, obtained by Veterans for Common Sense using the Freedom of Information Act.
9. William McMichael, "Gear Shortage Could Last Years After Iraq," *Army Times*, March 30, 2007.

The Future of GI Resistance

1. Zogby International, "U.S. Troops in Iraq: 72% Say End War in 2006," February 28, 2006, http://zogby.com/news/ReadNews.dbm?ID=1075.
2. Mary Wiltenburg, "When A Soldier in Iraq Won't Soldier," *Christian Science Monitor*, August 13, 2007.
3. The Appeal for Redress can be found at http://www.appealforredress.org.
4. Rick Maze, "End Iraq War, Service Members Tell Congress," *Marine Corps Times*, January 18, 2007.
5. Noah Schachtman, "Army Squeezes Soldier Blogs, Maybe to Death," *Wired*, May 2, 2007.

GLOSSARY OF MILITARY TERMS

.50-Caliber: A standard crew-served machine gun that fires .50-caliber rounds, often mounted on the top of a vehicle

AC-130 Gunship: Military fixed-wing aircraft used for close air support and force protection

ACR: Armored cavalry regiment

AK-47: A Russian-made assault rifle used by the many Iraqis, including the police, insurgents, and militias

Apache Helicopter: The U.S. Army's principal attack helicopter, flies in all weather, day and night

AWOL: Absent Without Leave

Battalion: A military unit of around five hundred to fifteen hundred men, usually consisting of between two and six companies, and typically commanded by a lieutenant colonel

Bradley Fighting Vehicle: An armored personnel carrier used to transport GIs and provide both medium and long-range firing capability for the infantry

CASH: Combat Support Hospital

CID: Criminal Investigation Division; police who investigate crimes inside the military

CO: Conscientious objector, someone who no longer believes in war because of religious, moral, or ethical reasons

CO: Commanding Officer

Company: A military unit, typically consisting of seventy-five to two hundred soldiers. Most companies are formed of three to five platoons

CPATT: Civilian Police Assistance Training Team, part of the U.S. occupation charged with training Iraqi police

DD214: U.S. military discharge certificate

Desertion: To abandon the military without permission

Division: A unit of the military typically consisting of between ten and twenty thousand troops

Flexi-cuffs: Plastic restraints used by soldiers to handcuff detainees

FOB: Forward Operating Base

Hillbilly Armor: Iraq war slang for homemade armor for soft-skinned Humvees

Humvee: Four-wheel-drive jeep used to patrol streets and transport troops, an acronyn for "High Mobility Multipurpose Wheeled Vehicle"

IED: Improvised explosive device

JAG: Judge Advocate General, the judicial arm of the U.S. military

Kalashnikov: An AK-47

KBR: Kellogg, Brown, and Root—a large civilian contractor operating in Iraq, subsidiary of Halliburton

KIA: Killed in action

M-16: A military issue assault rifle

M-60: A machine gun used by American forces

Mark 19: A belt-fed grenade launcher

MedEvac: Medical evacuation, from Iraq usually to Landstuhl Medical Center in Germany

Medic: A trained soldier who is responsible for providing first aid and frontline trauma care

Mortar: Fires shells at a much lower velocity and higher ballistic arc than other ordnance; their shells explode on impact with target

MP: Military police

MRE: Meal Ready to Eat, dehydrated food for troops in a combat zone

NCO: Noncommissioned officer, e.g., a sergeant

Peshmerga: Kurdish militia

Platoon: A military unit typically composed of two to four sections or squads and containing about thirty to fifty soldiers

PTSD: Post-Traumatic Stress Disorder

R&R: Rest and recreation, a short vacation soldiers are sometimes allowed to take during a deployment

RPG: Rocket-propelled grenade

SAPI Plates: Small arms protective inserts, ceramic armor plates used in vests to repel fragmentation and small arms fire

SMAW: A Shoulder-Launched Multipurpose Assault Weapon, a type of rocket launcher

TBI: Traumatic brain injury, physical brain damage

TRICARE: The military's health care plan

UCMJ: Uniformed Code of Military Justice, military law

APPENDIX

U.S ROE CARD

NOTHING ON THIS CARD PREVENTS YOU FROM USING DEADLY FORCE TO DEFEND YOURSELF.

1. Enemy military and paramilitary forces may be attacked subject to the following instructions:

a. Positive Identification (PID) is required prior to engagement. PID is 'reasonable certainty' that your target is a legitimate military target. If no PID, contact your next higher commander for decision.

b. Do not engage anyone who has surrendered or cannot fight due to sickness or wounds.

c. Do not target or strike any of the following except in self-defense to protect yourself, your unit, friendly forces, and designated persons or property under your control:

- Civilians
- Hospitals, mosques, churches, shrines, schools, museums, national monuments, and any other historical and cultural sites

d. Do not fire into civilian populated areas or buildings unless the hostile force is using them for hostile purposes or if necessary for your self-defense.

e. Minimize collateral damage.

2. You may use force, including deadly force, to defend yourself from persons who commit or are about to commit hostile acts against you. You may use the same level of force to protect the following:

- your unit, and other friendly forces (including Iraqi police and security forces).
- Enemy prisoners of war and detainees
- Civilians from crimes that are likely to cause death or serious bodily harm, such as murder or rape
- Designated organizations and/or property, such as personnel of the Red Cross/Red Crescent, UN, and US/UN supported organizations.

The official Rules of Engagement card issued to Sergeant Adam Kokesh
by the U.S. Marine Corps

Warning before firing
You may, time permitting, give a warning in a
loud clear voice.
    KIFF – ARMICK (Stop or I'll shoot)
    ERMY SE-LA-HAK (Drop your weapon)

3. **You may detain civilians if they interfere with
mission accomplishment, possess important
information, or if required for self-defense.**
    * Treat all persons and their property with
      respect and dignity.
    * Iraqi security forces and police are
      authorized to carry weapons.

4. **Necessary force, including deadly force, is
authorized for the protection of some types of
property including the following:**
    * Public utilities
    * Hospitals and public health facilities
    * Electric and Oil infrastructure
    * Coalition and captured enemy weapons and
      ammunition
    * Financial institutions
    * Other mission essential property designated by
      your commander

REMEMBER
    * Attack only hostile forces and military targets.
    * Avoid fratricide—be aware of nearby units and
      Iraqi police and security forces
    e. Spare civilians and civilian property, if
       possible.
    f. Do not loot or steal.
    g. Conduct yourself with dignity and honor.
    h. Comply with the Law of War. If you see a
       violation, report it.
    i. YOU ALWAYS HAVE THE RIGHT TO
       USE NECESSARY FORCE, INCLUDING
       DEADLY FORCE, TO PROTECT
       YOURSELF AND OTHERS.

These ROE will remain in effect until your commander

ACKNOWLEDGMENTS

Jose Vasquez for IVAW

J ose Vasquez represented IVAW in the testimonial editing process for this book and led the verification team on the Winter Soldier organizing committee. He served fourteen years in the U.S. Army and Army Reserve and was honorably discharged in May 2007 as a conscientious objector. Currently he is a PhD candidate in Cultural Anthropology at the Graduate Center, City University of New York (CUNY), where he is conducting research on the politics of veteran status in contemporary American society.

. . .

Winter Soldier: Iraq and Afghanistan was a grassroots effort in the truest sense of the word. Hundreds of family members, friends, and allies donated their time, energy, and money to ensure the voices of veterans were heard during four historic days in March 2008. On behalf of Iraq Veterans Against the War, I want to thank everyone that contributed to getting testifiers to the event and ensuring they were supported throughout the process. Your dedication made all the difference in this important endeavor.

To our family in Vietnam Veterans Against the War and Veterans for Peace, we are truly honored to stand on your shoulders. You all started a tradition in 1971 of veterans coming home and telling the truth about war;

we thought it was important to continue that tradition. You are all warriors for peace. To our loved ones in Military Families Speak Out, Gold Star Families for Peace, and Gold Star Families Speak Out, we thank you for walking with us as we bear the burden of war together.

Many, many allies offered their skills and expertise toward this momentous effort. To our co-author Aaron Glantz, thank you for your tenacity and deep understanding of our experiences. We've learned as much from you as you have from us. It's been a journey, my friend. Thanks to Ngoc for letting us steal you for weeks at a time.

Thanks to John Stauber for helping to make the right connections. Anthony Arnove, thanks for having the vision to publish these testimonies and the patience to put up with our drama. Julie Fain, thank you for your attention to detail. Jared Rodriguez, thanks for capturing us in the best possible light. And Tony Swofford, your words and empathetic ear are greatly appreciated. Thanks to Gerald Nicosia for your enthusiastic support. Ron Kovic, thank you for your powerful statement of support.

To the Winter Soldier organizing committee, your professionalism and dedication are immeasurable. For those of us in IVAW who know the humble beginnings of this whole process, we can read these lines and smile. Thanks to Fernando Braga, Aaron Hughes, and Liam Madden for their vision and infectious motivation. Thank you, gentlemen, for getting the ball rolling and giving the strategy team a boot in the ass.

Ally team: Jethro Heiko, Susie Husted, Matt Daloisio, Matt Smucker, Lori Hurlebaus, Joseph Gainza, Saif Rahman, Ward Reilly, and Nico Amador managed our numerous relationships with allies that were our "force-multipliers."

A/V and Web team: Danya Abt, Nick Jehlen, and Dan Summer helped make us presentable in audio, video, and digital formats. I can only imagine the hours you all put in.

Fundraising team: Amadee Braxton kept her watchful eye on the bottom line and fundraised like a champion.

Logistics team: Lily Hughes, Catherine Miller, Amy Meyer, and Lynn Phares did an amazing job making sure we had everything we needed and handled angry veterans with grace. Thanks to Lori Hurlebaus for maintaining order behind the scenes. Special thanks goes to Barry Romo, Ken Nielsen, and Bill Branson of our security detail; your efforts were instrumental in maintaining the "safe space" that we promised our testifiers. Thanks to Ryan Harvey and all the musicians, especially The Nightwatchman!

Media team: Emilie Surrusco and the whole media team took on a tremendous task and reached our strategic goal of coverage in the military media. Thanks to Francesca Lo Basso, Doyle Canning, Susie Husted, Ward Reilly, Geoff Millard, Matt Smucker, Vida Mia Ruiz, Lisa Cantu, Jane Song, Selena Coppa, Matt Daloisio, Nan Levinson, Nick Martin, Sarah Hirsch, Uruj Sheikh, Becca Rast, Saif Rahman, Adam Navarro-Lowery, Alain Jehlen, Charlie Anderson, Michael Applegate, and Suren Moodliar.

To the many journalists and filmmakers who took the time to listen, we say thanks. Thanks to Ariel Leve and Nina Berman for their story in the Sunday *New York Times Magazine*. For extended live, international coverage, special thanks to Amy Goodman (*Democracy Now!*); Aaron Glantz, Aimee Allison, and Esther Manilla (Pacifica—KPFA); Brian Drolet (Deep Dish TV); and everyone at Free Speech TV. For filming our forthcoming official documentary, thanks to Dave Zeiger (Displaced Films), Lenny Rotman (Northern Lights Productions), and their production teams. Thanks to Ric Rowley and Jacquie Soohen (Big Noise Films); and Matt Renner and Maya Schenwar (Truthout.org) for their coverage and support. And many, many more.

Outreach team: Aaron Hughes, Adrienne Kinne, Lovella Calica, Selena Coppa, Robert Clack, and all the regional coordinators were instrumental in reaching veterans and GIs with stories to tell.

Testimonial team: Perry O'Brien led the team with passion and focus. He had the unenviable task of selecting who would testify onstage.

Civilian testimony: Fernando Braga helped bring the stories of Iraqi and Afghan civilians to the table. Thanks to Alive in Baghdad (Brian Conley, Steve Wyshywaniuk, Omar Abdullah, Hayder Fahad, Isam Rasheed, Ahmad Muhammad, Firas Ekal) and Joan Seckler for risking your lives to collect and translate the Iraqi testimony. Also thanks to Dave Enders and Alaa Majeed for help with the translations.

Legal team: Kathy Gilberd, Michael Siegel, and Jeff Lake ensured our testifiers had the legal support they needed. Thanks to James Branum, J.E. McNeil, Dan O'Connor, and Jim Klimaski.

Mental health: Nancy Goldner, Ginny Hughes, Johanna (Hans) Buwalda, and Ray Parrish provided and organized professional mental health support.

Peer support: Adam Kokesh, Jeff Key, Tina Richards, Eric Estenzo, Resistance, and the whole peer support team kept us sane. Thanks to all the team coordinators, Bill Main, T.J. Buonomo, Toby Hartbarger, Rick Duncan, Mike Totten, Mike Marceau, and Frank Radosin; and to the Vietnam vets whose presence kept the lid on things for all their brothers and sisters in the audience, Bill Perry, Thomas Brinson, Elliot Adams, and Doug Ryder.

Ally panels: Martin Smith organized our ally panels, which helped provide context for our stories. Adrienne Kinne helped secure speakers as well. Jen Hogg and Patty McCann took the lead on the gender and sexuality panel. Our deepest gratitude goes to all our excellent panelists for their insights and unwavering support.

Verification team: Thanks to all our volunteers that did legwork on the verification process: Chere Krakovsky, Hannah Wolfe, Carlos Harris, Fabian Bouthillette, Luis C. Montalvan, Al Stolzer, Aimara Lin, Chris Lombardi, Elaine Brower, Kevin Huyge, Melissa Morrone, and Uruj Sheikh. Nick Martin was a real trooper interning with me on the verification team. Selena Coppa, Brandon Day, Ryan Johnson, Adam Kokesh, Patty McCann, Ryan McCarthy, Kenyon Ralph, Jim Reddin, and Hart Viges helped collect testimony. Special thanks go to Tanya Austin and Jason Wallace for taking up the slack in collecting on-site testimony.

Most importantly, to our brothers and sisters who offered testimony. Your bravery and sincerity are commendable. You trusted us with the deepest parts of your souls. You are all true patriots and our world is a better place because of the work you do. Let's continue to struggle together to end the suffering these wars and occupations have caused.

ACKNOWLEDGMENTS

Aaron Glantz

I am very grateful to all the brave veterans who shared their stories at Winter Soldier. Special thanks to former staff sergeant and IVAW board member Jose Vasquez, who spearheaded the difficult three-way negotiations between myself, Haymarket Books, and IVAW to make this book happen and then worked long and hard with little compensation both on the Winter Soldier verification team and on the nuts and bolts of this book. I'm also grateful to Jose and his wife Emi who allowed me to set up shop in their spare room for weeks on end while we cranked the book out. I'll try not to make such a mess next time. Thanks also to Perry O'Brien, Aaron Hughes, and Luis Carlos Montalvan. Thanks to Julie Fain and Anthony Arnove at Haymarket for rushing to get this book out before the November 2008 election. Thanks to my agent Michael Bourret at Dystel and Goderich Literary Management for understanding that we have do work sometimes even though it doesn't make the most money. Thanks to Gerald Nicosia, Penny Coleman, and John Stauber for their inspiration and support and to photographers Jared Rodriguez and Mike Hastie for their arresting images.

Thanks to Sasha Lilley at KPFA for green-lighting Pacifica Radio's historic, three-day live broadcast of Winter Soldier, which laid the groundwork for this book. Thanks to the rest of my broadcast team: Aimee

Allison, Esther Manilla, and Jon Almielah, with whom I shared this most important experience. Your professionalism, dedication, intelligence, and compassion are unmatched. In addition to your great work, I am grateful for your friendship and support. Thanks for helping me cry over this material and keeping me from quitting this difficult but important task. Thanks to therapist Rachel Erwin for donating her services.

Thanks to the other editors who published my freelance articles on Winter Soldier, who got the story out and kept me paid while I made my way through this labor of love: Katherine Stapp, Jeffrey Allen, David Barsamian, Monica Lopez, Tena Rubio, Harold Myerson, Andrew Lam, Joshua Holland, and Emily Schwartz-Greco. Thanks to Dal Lamanga, Jack Sawyer, and Historians Against the War for their generous support of this project. Thanks to Investigative Reporters and Editors for granting this project a Freelancer Fellowship Award.

Thanks to journalists Esther Manilla and Sarah Olson for helping me slog through these transcripts and for giving me such good advice about how to proceed. Thanks to Dahr Jamail and Salam Talib for being with me in Iraq and also at Winter Soldier. We are in the very unique space of seeing this war from both sides of the gun. It is a very difficult place to be, but the bridge we can build is very important. Salam, I will always remember running over to your scooter and giving you a giant hug as we signed off the air as Winter Soldier concluded.

Finally, but most importantly, I owe a deep debt of gratitude to my wife Ngoc Nguyen for her unconditional love. Thanks for understanding the mission I have taken on these last five years and for encouraging me to continue when I get discouraged. You worry about me enough but not too much. Thanks for all the "processing." I appreciate it more than I let on.

CONTRIBUTOR BIOGRAPHIES

About Iraq Veterans Against the War

Iraq Veterans Against the War (IVAW) was founded by Iraq War veterans in July 2004 at the annual convention of Veterans for Peace (VFP) in Boston to give a voice to the large number of active-duty servicemembers and veterans who are against the Iraq War, but are under various pressures to remain silent. From its inception, IVAW has called for:

- Immediate withdrawal of all occupying forces in Iraq;

- Reparations for the human and structural damages Iraq has suffered, and stopping the corporate pillaging of Iraq so that their people can control their own lives and future; and

- Full benefits, adequate health care (including mental health), and other supports for returning servicemen and women.

Our membership includes recent veterans and active-duty servicemembers from all branches of the military service, National Guard members, and reservists who have served in the U.S. military since September 11, 2001. IVAW's strategy is to mobilize the military community to withdraw its support for the war and occupation in Iraq.

Today, IVAW members are in forty-eight states, Washington, D.C., Canada, and on numerous bases overseas, including Iraq. IVAW supports all those resisting the war, including conscientious objectors and others facing military prosecution for their refusal to fight. IVAW advocates for full funding for the Department of Veterans Affairs, and full quality health treatment (including mental health) and benefits for veterans when they return from duty.

About Aaron Glantz

Aaron Glantz is an independent journalist whose work has appeared in the *Nation*, the *Progressive*, the *San Francisco Chronicle*, the *American Prospect*, *Forbes*, Alternet, and on *Democracy Now!* and *Yahoo! News*. In addition to *Winter Soldier*, he is author of the *San Francisco Chronicle* bestseller *How America Lost Iraq* (Tarcher/Penguin) and the forthcoming *The War Comes Home: Washington's Battle Against America's Veterans* (University of California Press).

Aaron reported extensively inside Iraq from 2003 to 2005 and has been covering veterans' issues since his return to the United States. He the recipient of a Project Censored Award, an Investigative Reporters and Editors Freelancer Fellowship Award, and a California Journalism Award. He is currently a Fellow at the Carter Center's Mental Health Program and the Hechinger Institute at Columbia University Teachers College.

About Anthony Swofford

Anthony Swofford served in a U.S. Marine Corps Surveillance and Target Acquisition/Scout-Sniper platoon during the Gulf War. After the war, he was educated at American River College, the University of California, Davis, and the University of Iowa Writers' Workshop. He is author of *Jarhead: A Marine's Chronicle of the Gulf War and Other Battles* and the novel *Exit: A Novel*. He lives in New York.

About Jared Rodriguez

Jared Rodriguez is a documentary photographer, military family member, and activist living in New York City. He is currently working on a portrait project about antiwar activists, veterans, and military family members. He can be reached at www.jaredrodriguez.com.

About Mike Hastie

Mike Hastie served as a U.S. Army Medic in Vietnam from 1970 to 1971. He says that when he photographed the anger, anguish, grief, and sense of betrayal visible in testifiers at Winter Soldier, he felt like he was taking pictures of his own PTSD and the trauma of his fellow Vietnam veterans.

ABOUT HAYMARKET BOOKS

Haymarket Books is a nonprofit, progressive book distributor and publisher, a project of the Center for Economic Research and Social Change. We take inspiration and courage from our namesakes, the Haymarket Martyrs, who gave their lives fighting for a better world. Their 1886 struggle for the eight-hour day, which gave us May Day, the international workers' holiday, reminds workers around the world that ordinary people can organize and struggle for their own liberation. These struggles continue today across the globe—struggles against oppression, exploitation, hunger, and poverty.

ALSO FROM HAYMARKET BOOKS

Beyond the Green Zone:
Dispatches from an Unembedded Journalist in Occupied Iraq

The critically acclaimed, indispensable account of life in Iraq under U.S. occupation, now with a new afterword. ISBN 978-1-931859-61-5.

Road from ar-Ramadi: The Private Rebellion of Staff Sergeant Camilo Mejía

Camilo Mejía with a foreword by Chris Hedges • A courageous, personal account of rebellion within the ranks of the U.S. military in wartime—written by the first soldier to publicly refuse to return to fight in Iraq. ISBN: 978-1-931859-553-0.

Winter Soldiers: An Oral History of the Vietnam Veterans Against the War

Richard Stacewicz • This is the story of the soldiers who spoke their conscience and helped end the war in Vietnam. 978-1-931859-60-8

War Without End: The Iraq War in Context

Michael Schwartz • In this razor-sharp analysis, TomDispatch.com commentator Michael Schwartz demolishes the myths used to sell the U.S. public the idea of an endless "war on terror. 978-1-931859-54-7.

Vietnam: The (Last) War the U.S. Lost

Joe Allen • This history from below analyzes the impact of the war in Vietnam on the region and its people, as well as on American workers, students, and politicians, and discusses the relationship between the era's antiwar, labor, and civil rights movements. ISBN: 978-1-931859-49-3.

Blackwater (Español)

Jeremy Scahill • The New York Times bestseller and scathing exposé now in Spanish, in a fully updated edition. ISBN: 978-1-931859-62-2.